With
Scripture
as My
COMPASS

Peter —

With God as your guide
and friendship as your constant
Companion, I wish you
TRAVELING MERCiES on your
life Journey:

ENJoy THE Journey
KNOW THAT God LoVES you
RETURN Home SAFELY

With loving (3yr.)
Anniversary wishes,

Becky
9.29.04

With Scripture as My Compass

Meditations for the Journey

THOMAS EHRICH

Abingdon Press
Nashville

WITH SCRIPTURE AS MY COMPASS
MEDITATIONS FOR THE JOURNEY

Copyright © 2004 by Thomas L. Ehrich

All rights reserved.

This book is printed on acid-free paper.

Library of Congress Cataloging-in-Publication Data

Ehrich, Thomas L.
  With Scripture as my compass : meditations for the journey / Thomas Ehrich.
    p. cm.
  Includes index.
  ISBN 0-687-03811-1 (binding : adhesive, perfect : alk. paper)
  1. Bible. N.T. Gospels—Meditations.   2. Christian life—Biblical teaching.   I. Title.
  BS2555.54.E75 2004
  242'.5—dc22

                                                                              2004016085

04 05 06 07 08 09 10 11 12 13—10 9 8 7 6 5 4 3 2 1

MANUFACTURED IN THE UNITED STATES OF AMERICA

*T*o My Wife, Heidi

Contents

Introduction

[Jesus said,] "I am the living bread that came down from heaven. Whoever eats of this bread will live forever; and the bread that I will give for the life of the world is my flesh." (John 6:51)

We should be buying an ark," says my wife, as another rainstorm drenches central North Carolina. Instead, it is car-shopping day. Armed with data and a carefully culled list of possibilities, we head off to test-drive four cars. Later, armed with a spreadsheet and our best approximation of rational intent, we make a decision that works for both of us.

I then lie awake with "buyer's remorse." Not about the cost, for the bottom line isn't much changed, but about practicality. What use is a two-seater to a family man? Don't worry, says my wife. No car is forever. If it doesn't work out, we trade it in. For cars, as romantic as they seem, are commodities.

We yearn for the eternal, for something that doesn't get washed away in the rains of life. Homes come and go. Favorite bedrooms pass to others. Loved ones die. Friendships don't survive moving. Jobs are easily lost and changed, marriages can die, hopes and dreams can rust. Cars rust, too.

In our search for the eternal, many turn to God, and rightly so. For when you cut through the momentary passions of religion, God promises to be enduring, with a love that can outlast our waywardness, a steadfastness that can survive our turning to other gods, and an overarching purpose that isn't bound by human pride. Jesus said his life would open the door to larger life. "Whoever eats of this bread will live forever."

What did he mean? For two thousand years, the church has seen itself as custodian of holy bread, managing the process by which pilgrims seek and receive official bread. Eucharist became a ritual. The church defined what it meant, who could receive it, and who should be sent away empty. In an age of superstition, the wafer was deemed to have magical properties. Excommunication was a mortal threat. Even now, in non-eucharistic traditions, the religious see themselves as custodians of the holy, as called to determine who wins eternal life or eternal fire.

We need to be clear about what Jesus said. He didn't establish an institution, he didn't create orders of ministry, he didn't create rituals, he didn't anoint a cadre of gate-keepers to bar the unworthy. Jesus said, "I am the living bread," and "the bread that I will give for the life of the world is my flesh." Jesus gave his life, not an instruction manual.

Maybe that life resides for a time in the offerings of religion, as romance and adventure occasionally reside in a car or house. But many words spoken centuries ago in utter certainty have been revealed as self-serving, time-bound, or simply wrong. Leaders who claimed to hold the keys to eternal life had only a passing moment, and way too much vainglory. Nothing lasted, not even the grandest structures or purest intentions. Despite our arguing and clinging, words change, better translations emerge, new songs erupt, new structures offer equivalent or better glimpses of the holy, and always new assignments pour over us.

This is painful for church folk like ourselves to see. Like a beloved family home being left behind, or a car rusting and sputtering, the supposed verities of religion pass away. It is a sad and confusing time, and we seem mired in the stresses that sadness and confusion create.

What I wish is that church communities could see the eternal, as Jesus hoped we would see it. No longer in structures and inherited verities that we defend against modernity, but in the Lord himself, in the person and promise of Jesus, in the difficult work of learning through parables, dying to self, living as pilgrims, and seeing ourselves as servants, no longer as masters or consumers.

Jesus promised exactly what we yearn for. But first we need to get out of our own way.

My aim in this book is to help us get out of our own way. Think how much of our religious energy in recent memory has gone into fighting and into staying afloat. Like managers of a failing restaurant, we have fought over locations and furnishings, written new menus, added items that we thought would appeal, blamed chef and staff, rearranged tables, vowed to be friendlier, and hired an army of consultants.

Yesterday's denominational winners have watched momentum pass to other franchises and wondered if they should change course. Or is the new trend an aberration and we just need to hold on until the "golden age" returns?

Questions pile on questions, leadership groups agonize long into the night, academics seek better theories for helping would-be clergy to succeed, and the half-empty look longingly at the full and are both aghast at what it takes to fill the pews and envious of those who accomplish fullness. Meanwhile, the world at large increasingly shrugs off religion as uninteresting. People discover that finding faith and knowing God aren't synonymous with the survival of religious institutions. Seekers can pursue a relationship with God without entering a church door. They can read Scripture on their own and develop a robust faith outside the creeds and folkways of traditional religion. That is difficult for church leaders to imagine, and they tend to scoff at alternative forms of sustenance. But as pews get emptier and the most visible religious energy comes from single-cause zealots staking their shrill claim to truth, reasonable believers start to wonder if franchise management is indeed their calling.

People, you see, seek God because of something deep inside, and God seeks people out of a love that defies packaging. Neither form of seeking requires the church as institution. God's determination to love all that God has made isn't bound by the church's rules or barriers or theologies. Humanity's yearnings can't be channeled into obedience to institutional imperatives.

My aim is to help people experience God through the power of stories. Stories aren't theories or theologies. Stories are glimpses. The aim of stories isn't to sway opinion or to recruit followers, but to encourage seeing. No story is complete in itself, no story speaks to every person, no story is free of ambiguity. Our earliest ancestors in faith were storytellers. Jesus was a storyteller.

It is time, I think, that we abandoned our two-thousand-year quest for perfect law, perfect interpretation, and perfect structure. I don't believe God values such a quest. Nor is it within our grasp. It is time we stepped back from institutional-survival issues and stepped forward as storytellers in a troubled world, as servants and door openers, as companions to the broken, as far more humble and uncertain than our creeds suggest us to be, more like pilgrims than experts.

PART ONE

Certainty

Versus

Uncertainty

Faith has long sought certainty.

But it is better to live boldly in uncertainty.

Easter

Mark 16:8: So they went out and fled from the tomb, for terror and amazement had seized them; and they said nothing to anyone, for they were afraid.

I want music this Easter morning. Not the trumpet of muscular Christianity, but the oboe—melancholy and yet floating, somber and yet capable of dancing—a sound suitable for an empty tomb whose message isn't yet known. Not the grand pipe organ of triumphant Christianity, but the horn—hard to play, sometimes lost in the symphony's full sound and yet unmistakable by itself—a sound suitable for not knowing where to take one's confusing discovery. Not the massed choirs of large Christianity, but the alto voice, the voice that transcends gender and adds harmony to the melody—a voice suitable for walking in pairs.

I think of going to church this Easter Day. But I feel distanced from trumpets, grand sounds, full pews. Not that there is anything unseemly about such grandeur. I am walking a different road this year. That's all. This is Mark's road, I think, an Easter Gospel that begs no shouts of triumph, but simply ends in "terror and amazement."

From other sources, the rest of Easter became known. But Mark says nothing of such outcomes. Did Mark not know the rest of the story, or was Mark urging the faithful to stay longer in the emptiness?

Mark doesn't preach as readily as other accounts. Many preachers today, in fact, will go straight to "Easter triumph, Easter joy," to Paul's vision of the Risen Christ "seated at the right hand of God" and of believers sharing his "glory." With one's flock dressed up and eager, it is the rare preacher who will speak of "terror and amazement," of a message so confusing that the first witnesses dared not tell it to anyone, not yet. Or if they dare that road, it will be at a Vigil, where silence is valued and won't disturb the day's festivities.

I have done my share of triumphant shouts. I remember one year, being so moved by trumpets and voices that I literally screamed the Easter acclamation, "Alleluia! Christ is risen!" I thought I knew the full story, and I considered it worthy of shouting. I was well wrapped in the mantle of the church and its abiding convictions.

And yet, even amid the shouting, I sometimes preached about the empty tomb, not the full sanctuary. Even then, I sensed that we were missing something. Not that our creeds were erroneous, but that faith's assertion—"On the third day he rose again"— hadn't yet been fully understood.

I think we need to stay longer in Mark's Easter moment— empty tomb, confusing words, not knowing what to do next, afraid to talk, asking God for guidance, for courage to move.

> *I think we need to stay longer in Mark's Easter moment—empty tomb, confusing words, not knowing what to do next, afraid to talk, asking God for guidance, for courage to move.*

I don't think the rising of Jesus was a precursor to an institution's triumph. It was victory over darkness and death. It was victory won by self-emptying. It was a call to go, but not the naming of destination. It was the first step on a journey into the not-yet-known, not to be heralded by the trumpet fanfare of triumphant arrival, but to be serenaded by the subtler oboe of beckoning.

And so, while coffee is brewing, I say my prayers. I ask for guidance and pray for my family, who are scattered this weekend. Then I turn on the radio and am greeted by an oboe duet, a concerto for horn, and Bach's painstaking blending of many voices.

Bach knew trumpets, but in the slow orchestral movement of his *Easter Oratorio*, it is the horns that lead the way and beckon the trumpets to sing. If I were to guess what God is doing in our midst, I would say that God is beckoning us, not crowning us.

8

Shoes

John 20:20-21: [Jesus] showed them his hands and his side. Then the disciples rejoiced when they saw the Lord. Jesus said to them again, "Peace be with you. As the Father has sent me, so I send you."

Their return flight is five hours late, but now the flight-listing board glows red, "Arrived." I put down my book and assume the position. Prior to September 11, 2001, I could have greeted my wife and youngest son at their arrival gate. I could have seen them emerge from the tunnel, their heads bobbing in the line of disembarking passengers, our eyes meeting, smiles erupting. Now, with security tightened, greeters must wait at the bottom of an escalator near baggage claim. Arriving passengers descend from above, appearing feet first.

All manner of shoes and legs come into view. It's better to see eyes, for eyes can sparkle no matter what age, weight, or scuffing has wrought. But shoes and legs it is, so I look for young-boy legs, sneakers and shorts. There they are! I move forward to greet my family. They see me. My son rushes forward. We smile, we hug, and now we are one again.

Back in New Hampshire, they left a hole in other lives. In rejoining this family, they left another family. The kitchen table where they sat is emptier now. They are emptier, too, wishing as always that career and life choices hadn't taken us so far from loved ones.

Faith is in many ways a tragic affair. We must believe in that which we cannot see. We must accept incompleteness, the time of not-yet, or as a friend is putting it in a poem, "Between."

But faith most disturbs in starting us on a cycle of sending and going, arriving and leaving, knowing and not knowing, feeling whole and broken, seeing and not seeing, rejoicing and lament-

9

ing, recognizing and doubting. Once we choose to embrace the possibility of freedom and hope, we become like the Hebrews crossing the sea. We must leave behind what we know, not only the sins and despair that we are happy to leave behind, but also settledness, roots, certainty, the very homes which gave us birth.

Jesus came into the lives of several dozen men and women and then departed. He could have escaped trial, but he chose to confront the darkness. They watched him being dragged off to suffer and to die.

Now he was back among them! They rejoiced. But they couldn't cling to him. The moment was brief. Not only must he leave again, but also now he was sending them off, away from each other. They would walk different roads, but carry the same crosses, suffer the same rejection, endure the same cycles of arriving and leaving.

> We have wanted to freeze Easter, rather than embrace Easter.

Jesus bade them look at his hands and side, where nails and spear had torn flesh. Not his eyes, which could deceive, but the marks of suffering.

Christians rush to declare victory—"The strife is o'er, the battle won"—but, in fact, the strife was just beginning. Like a bride and groom leaving homes to start new life, disciples must leave everything behind to follow faith's command.

Christianity has tended to avoid departures and therefore to be rigid, with rigid rules, rigid doctrines, rigid practices. We fight change, and when we do change, it is always too slowly to keep pace with God's restless spirit. We have wanted to freeze Easter, rather than embrace Easter. We have wanted to see Jesus' eyes, as if his arrival were a rekindling of something lost.

Instead, like me standing below an escalator scanning shoes and legs, Jesus bids us see his hands and side. For that must be our future—arriving and leaving, holding and losing, dancing at the Reed Sea and hungering in the wilderness, never quite home, never seeing fully, always between.

Focus

John 12:23-24: Jesus answered them, "The hour has come for the Son of Man to be glorified. Very truly, I tell you, unless a grain of wheat falls into the earth and dies, it remains just a single grain; but if it dies, it bears much fruit."

Relatively few people attend this afternoon's plenary session of the software users conference. The cavernous hall feels empty, as if a better party were happening elsewhere. I don't think no-shows are uninterested in the future direction of the software we use and implement, or blasé about achievement awards. I just think it's hard to focus here.

The resort environment of Disney World says, "Play!" The gargantuan images and perfected vistas steadily erode one's sense of reality. Wars seem far away. Phone calls with family get filtered through controlled air. Questions that seemed pertinent to conference planners feel small and drab.

Focus is elusive. Focus requires pressure, felt need, discomfort, crisis, even danger. This resort is designed to prevent any of those conditions from occurring. Everything works, everyone smiles, every appetite has been anticipated, every hazard has been removed, every distraction has been banished. The only questions that break the surface here have to do with what to eat, see, or buy next. These aren't complaints. I suppose we all need a break from time to time. But I know it's time to leave. For sugar isn't a meal.

Perhaps the most difficult stage in the ministry of Jesus came when he said it was time to leave. The party, as it were, was over. The pleasing routines of walking about, learning together, and winning adherents needed to end. For the longer he stayed, the more elusive focus would become. He would become like this resort: larger than life, distanced from reality, a banquet that had no valences to the outside, too tidy, too confined, too comfortable, too easy.

He needed to "fall into the earth," he told them. He needed to suffer and to die. Through his suffering, he needed to fling wide the gates to reality, to the hungry, bewildered, and bedraggled, to those still walking in darkness and to those profiting from that darkness. Jesus needed to reopen their minds to the questions, rather than draw them deeper into the comfort of answers.

This was a hard time for his followers. They didn't welcome these open gates, and nearly all refused to walk through them. They preferred the "resort," where decisions about eating, seeing, and buying seemed enough.

By the time Jesus fell to earth, he was alone. Before his resurrection was many days old, his followers were trying to re-create the resort and its pleasing vistas.

In a sense, the Christianization of Rome and the subsequent institution-building were the first Disney adventures. The grand cathedrals of Europe were the Magic Kingdoms of their age. The closed canon of the New Testament, the closed circles of the "saved," the closed doors of the monasteries, the closed ranks of denominations, the perfected vistas and hushed venues were efforts to escape the world, to create places where ambiguities and intrusions were filtered out.

> We need to ask what it cost Jesus to leave the party.

We need to ask what it cost Jesus to leave the party. What depth of self-awareness enabled him to comprehend the danger of success? What depth of self-denial enabled him to walk away at the very moment he could be crowned king? What depth of self-emptying enabled him to put down the heaping plate of resort food, to turn his back on the tidy confines his followers would be happy to create, to stride past the guarded gates and out into a world where darkness was winning?

Instead of perfecting our vistas and arguing about the wording of our menus, perhaps we, too, should leave the resort and return to the world. What we have created is nice, but sugar still isn't a meal.

Suffer

John 10:11: Jesus said, "I am the good shepherd. The good shepherd lays down his life for the sheep."

She survived her childhood, but now, as an adult, she struggles to survive the incest that ruled her youth. She prayed hard, says a friend, but God evidently "didn't hear her," because the abuse kept happening. Where was God?

Now she is studying yet another of those books that proclaim God as in control of all things, as one who answers all prayer, as one who leads all faithful people to abundance. Now, in addition to memories of incest, she must face the cruel implication that God was in control of those nightly visits, that God chose to ignore her cries, that she must have been insufficiently faithful.

I remember trying to pastor a group of incest survivors. It was so difficult to imagine life across that divide, so difficult to sit within their pain, so difficult to stay in the circle as they raged against adults who betrayed trust, and as they sorted through popular religion's blithe assertion of a God who plans and controls. What sort of God would have a "plan" that required a child's abuse?

The image of God as planner, controller and dispenser of prayer rewards is a pleasing conceit for the healthy and prosperous. It is pleasing to think of their good fortune as divine favor. But what about the rest of us? Other than asking them to leave, what do the abundance-seekers have to say to the unfortunate, the abused, the weak, the lost, the vast majority who cannot wake up each morning thanking God for a full larder?

"Winners pray harder"—is that godly counsel? "Cooperate with God to make abundance happen"—does that do anything more than sell books?

My friend asks how to help her friend. The first answer, of course, is to love her, to stay beside her, to listen to her as deeply as possible. Religion tends to have a short attention span for pain. Don't be like that.

You can also say this, I respond: "Yes, God did hear her, and God wept for her. She couldn't hear the sound of God's weeping then, but can she hear it now? For the truth about God seems to be that God suffers as much as we do from a fundamental decision to allow creation to be free."

I don't say such things lightly. Another friend asked recently, "If God isn't in control, then what is God?" Many people have built their faith around God as planner and controller.

> *The image of God as planner, controller, and dispenser of prayer rewards is a pleasing conceit for the healthy and prosperous.*

Jesus said, "I am the good shepherd. The good shepherd lays down his life for the sheep." The good shepherd doesn't cause the wolf to attack, or compel the "hired hand" to be lazy and inattentive, or see the attack coming and yet allow it to happen in order to teach some spiritual lesson. Evil does its own work.

God is a binder of wounds. God weeps over the fallen, as Jesus wept over Jerusalem. God suffers with creation, as Jesus suffered when his friend Lazarus died. God points the way to good pasture, but whether we err and stray is up to us.

God established a good creation, but whether we farm it wisely and share its fruits with others is up to us. If the few prosper while the many starve, that isn't a divine abundance plan at work, but "man's inhumanity to man."

It isn't "God's will" that sets parent against child, or race against race, or predators against the weak, or the selfish against everyone. It is God's will to bear the suffering of God's people, to suffer with them, to shine light into the darkness, and when the darkness fights back, to lay down his life on the cross.

Simplicity

John 10:16: Jesus said, "So there will be one flock, one shepherd."

As I complete another round of golf, I marvel at my passion for a game that largely eludes me. Golf offers a form of simplicity, I think. Golf's swing mechanics and rituals are complex. But for these hours, all other complexities stand aside. Hit the ball, follow the shot, hit again, don't stew.

Such a welcome contrast to other things. Earlier today, for example, we attended a soccer game, at which opposing players shoved, tripped, elbowed, and cursed, while their parents exhorted them to greater violence.

After golf, I visit our house site, expecting to find kitchen countertops completely installed, as promised. Instead, I discover that the countertop crew never showed. I leave a vehement voice mail for the installer. Golf's simple pleasures are forgotten.

Golf, of course, is totally artificial. For life is a complex affair, from beginning to end. We discover our toes, we discover our parents, we discover other people, we discover ourselves in the context of other people, we discover dangers, we discover our limits, we discover humankind's astonishing capacity for cruelty, we discover mortality—one layer of discovery on top of another, while we struggle to comprehend.

At some point, if we are fortunate, we discover God. Or God discovers us. But somehow we become aware that there is more to life than we can see, there is hope that we don't invent, there is love that we cannot dampen. Such discovery happens at every critical life stage.

Humankind's consistent instinct upon discovering God is to seek the complexities of religion. It's like organized soccer: instead of allowing kids to kick balls around, we form leagues, rules, and schedules. Religion tends to be dominated by strong-willed soccer moms and dads, who want their child (idea, belief, preference) to succeed, even at the expense of others, who bristle at any interference (competing idea, competing preference), who want victory, because victory has become a measure of self-worth.

Religion thrives on layers of complexity. They stretch the mind, they provide employment, they make it seem unnecessary to go deeply into self or other, they provide cover for class warfare, ethnic pride and other forms of competition.

Because we find complexity so engaging, we conclude that God is complexity extended to the nth degree. Hence the extraordinary wordiness of most theology.

But what if God is the opposite? What if God is simplicity? What if God's original idea truly was a garden, in which friends could walk about freely? What if God wanted nothing more for humanity than a piece of land, and all the rest—codes, rituals, tribal consciousness—was humanity's equivalent of Adam's hiding?

> *What if God wanted nothing more for humanity than a piece of land, and all the rest—codes, rituals, tribal consciousness—was humanity's equivalent of Adam's hiding?*

What if Jesus had it figured out—walk about, touch lives, bring them into a circle where all are welcome, love extravagantly, one flock, one shepherd? What if all the rest—structures, hierarchies, theologies, traditions, denominations, right opinions, jealousies, warfare—was humanity's unbelief?

If God were simplicity, the "one flock" wouldn't be denominational supremacy, but a simple reality, namely, that God loves everything God has made. The "one shepherd" wouldn't be an institution's standard-bearer, but a simple reality, namely, that God cares for God's sheep.

When we heard "one flock, one shepherd," we wouldn't put on our evangelistic recruitment boots. We would look around and see each other as already loved and treasured. We wouldn't start another argument about whose opinions are best grounded in Scripture, tradition, reason, or force. We would rejoice at our piece of land and not need it to be normative for anyone else. Our "religion" would be "rely and connect," not "restrain and tie back." (Same Latin root, different outcomes.)

Instead of projecting our limits and complexity onto God, we would hear God searching for us, and we would ask why we are hiding.

Ministry

Mark 6:7: [Jesus] called the twelve and began to send them out two by two, and gave them authority over the unclean spirits.

Building a stone wall turns out to be hot, dirty work, but extraordinarily satisfying. It feels clever to dig out mower-eating rocks from our future lawn and to convert them into something useful. I tell my son that this is how his ancestors made farmable land in New Haven Colony.

Carrying the stones is one of those repetitive chores that free the mind to think about other things. As I cross the land, I begin to know its contours and to make it my home. Assembling stones is like working a jigsaw puzzle, except that the materials are forgiving.

In time, stones start their march across the ground. Various sizes, colors, and textures soon form a whole, as seen from a distance. As is usual with me, I start the work and then do the research. It turns out my intuition—mix the sizes, take care in fitting stones into crevices, test stability, work up to the largest—is on the mark.

Most satisfying is doing this work as a family. For this one day, we are like the family farmers way back in our heritage: mutually dependent, each contributing according to ability and strength. I think this is the way Jesus envisioned ministry. Disciples working together, deriving sustenance from the land, doing what they could, trying to fit human diversity into something new and life-giving.

Instead, Christians re-created the priestly caste of the Old Testament, with an ordained class operating in strict hierarchy, being named "ministers," and everyone else rendered an audience, an employer class, or when-it-is-convenient partners in ministry. When clergy have the upper hand, they order the laity about. When laity have the upper hand, clergy become hired hands.

We developed a taste for uniformity and perfection. Our stone walls had to be just so, as if only properly trained experts could tackle the important work, as if willingness and a good heart weren't enough. Members became monochromatic.

This overstates reality, but not by much. Consider mass defections from ordained employment, constant conflict in congregational leadership over who gets to tell the other what to do, and inconsistency in energy and performance.

Consider our concern for proper equipment—technology, clever leave-behinds for calls, training classes that promote ministry as requiring expertise, electronic gear that rivals rock shows.

Consider the loneliness of modern ministers, ordained or lay, as they prepare in solitude, serve in solitude, bear a community's pressure in solitude.

> We developed a taste for uniformity and perfection. Our stone walls had to be just so.

But then consider the times when we do it Jesus' way. Working side by side at church suppers and bazaars, building houses in teams, doing missionary work in teams, putting on renewal events in teams, handling crises in impromptu teams, laughing and crying together, deriving sustenance not from expertise but from each other—this is when joy is found, and this is when we accomplish something.

Jesus sent his disciples out in pairs, because the model for ministry isn't the paid expert driving alone to work, but the unsure deriving strength from each other. Jesus sent them out unequipped, because gear can be a crutch, tending to gear can be a substitute for ministry, and purchasing gear provides escape from the harder work of tending souls. Jesus told them to engage with the people, not to view them as a "market to be tapped," but as hosts, friends, colleagues. If friendship wasn't returned, move on, because ministry isn't something one can compel.

Our ineffective models for ministry are deeply ingrained— priestly caste, hierarchy grounded in expertise, some giving and others receiving, hired hands and those who employ them. They even have the weight of church law behind them. But they aren't working. Jesus gave us a better way.

Doctrine

Matthew 22:15: Then the Pharisees went and plotted to entrap [Jesus] in what he said.

My wife asks me to proofread an essay she has written. I read it carefully for errors of spelling and grammar, but not for what I might consider errors of thought. This essay expresses her thoughts, not mine. Even if I disagreed, it would be unethical to change her opinions to mine.

As for errors of fact, well, that might be a different matter. But even there, most observations about history and reality are just that, observations, in which the observer filters data through an idiosyncratic screen. Beyond a certain point—2 + 2 = 4, or the capitol of South Dakota is Pierre—fact can be elusive, especially when people and social phenomena are involved.

The foundation of intellect isn't factual accuracy, but freedom, including the freedom to be wrong, the freedom to see things differently from other people, the freedom to change one's mind, and most important, the freedom to arrive at one's own perceptions, thoughts, opinions, and conclusions.

That freedom is anathema to many Christians. From the earliest days, the Christian community has devoted enormous energy to defining a single correct way to believe. Theologians thought and bishops decided, and their product was doctrine: a single teaching on each subject, deemed the church's official teaching and a definitive insight into the mind of God. Any other conclusion, they believed, would violate the Almighty. Therefore, name the heresy and punish the heretic, lest weaker souls be led astray.

History hasn't been kind to most doctrines. Some were revealed as self-serving and political. Some were exposed by discoveries of better manuscripts. Some were exposed by science, that dread enemy of theological certainty. Some were grounded in controversies of the moment. Some doctrines simply stopped making sense.

The quest for certainty remains fervent, however, even desperate. In troubled and confusing times, as these most certainly are, many demand absolutes, and, with increasing shrillness, they demand silence from those who believe differently. They are especially offended by those who walk comfortably among uncertainties and who would reopen heretofore settled questions.

Rather than encourage people on their own journeys of discovery, many Christians want to correct the divergent. With Scripture citations flashing like sabers, they go for the "palpable hit" which will reveal error and lead to surrender. Failing that, they cite 2,000 years of Christian tradition or, more likely, the last ten years of "the way we always do things." The ground for argument keeps shifting, for the need to be right is desperate.

History hasn't been kind to most doctrines.

In such a quest for control, words are for entrapment, as the Pharisees tried with Jesus, not for encouragement. Words are for winning approval through conformity, not for playing with ideas, testing the boundaries of one's understanding, seeing new things, or learning about oneself. Words are weapons, and if they can prove your words wrong, then they win. That you might use words to make your own exploration of the wilderness means nothing to them.

When my wife holds out her words, she offers me a treasure. I must not abuse it. If I have any love and respect for her, I must protect her freedom to think and to express. Even if her thoughts threatened the very foundations of my worldview, I have no right to diminish her freedom.

Would that attitude, in theology, produce some loosey-goosey theories, some odd behavior, some violation of settled norms, some discomfort for the comfortable? Probably.

But look at what insistence on conformity and the enshrining of doctrine have produced: two thousand years of religious warfare, heresy trials, absurd doctrines defended by the sword, cruelty beyond measure, nonsensical resistance to the most basic discoveries of science, and a community divided by hatred and turned so thoroughly inward that the very conditions which drove Jesus to death on Calvary are hardly noticed.

Survive

*Matthew 22:16-17: So [the Pharisees] sent their disciples . . .
with the Herodians, saying . . . "Tell us, then, what you think.
Is it lawful to pay taxes to the emperor, or not?"*

L ong ago and far away, in the hospital nearest their Army
camp, my mother gave birth to her firstborn son. It was a
different world. Nations were coming out of a brutal war.
Allied troops were entering bleak camps in Germany and Poland
and discovering the fuller extent of Nazism's evil. West and East
were sharpening new swords to carve up Europe. Anyone near
Japan was gazing bleakly on a new form of mass destruction.

In a nation that was still largely rural, families were counting
the dead. In Italy, Britain, and other nations where bombs had
struck nightly, survivors had mountains of rubble to clear. In
Germany, a ravaged people had to confront moral collapse that
went beyond the usual mayhem of war.

A flood of energy was released into the world economy, especially in the relatively undamaged United States. Over the next
two decades, a massive shift of population occurred, not just the
"baby boom" of which I was an early arrival, but movement away
from farms and small towns and into cities and suburbs, where
only a few had survival skills.

Those were "quiet weeks," as Garrison Keillor says about his
"Lake Wobegon," at least for whites and those who exited the
war with their families, minds, and bodies reasonably intact.
Others became invisible, as if their realities and needs had fallen
off the table. A rising tide didn't lift all boats. Black soldiers
returned to Jim Crow. Women who had thrived in wartime jobs
were told to get back into the kitchen. Patriotic Appalachian
folks returned to coalfields of unimaginable deprivation.

We were dividing even then but becoming less able to per-
ceive ourselves. We were traumatized, I think, and wanted to see
only sun-dappled schoolrooms, happy families on leafy streets,

prosperous workers driving new Fords and Chevys, cheerful churches with crowded pews, sweet music about "young love, first love," and Ike in the White House.

Those scenes were real—I know, I lived them—but so were the scenes we didn't want to see. We were surprised when early glimpses of cultural angst appeared, marriages started collapsing, drugs became common, "Peggy Sue" got pregnant, and then came the 1960s and open cultural rebellion.

We were surprised when racial tensions boiled over and cities erupted. We were surprised when labor strife shut down mills, mines, and factories. We were surprised when church pews began to empty, around 1964.

Maybe it is impossible to see seeds before they sprout. Maybe reality is always a surprise, and the most we can expect of ourselves is nimble response to the uncontrollable.

> *We will pay our taxes to the emperor, as it were, and then learn to see the coin's holier context. It will always be a struggle and leave us bruised.*

Maybe we are always going to be survivors—surviving other people's poor decisions and our own, surviving cultural forces which wash over us, surviving the broad-flowing acid of injustice, surviving rapid changes which render our skills obsolete and public institutions bankrupt.

Our serenity and peace will come, I believe, from that very surviving. Victors become spoiled. The privileged become soft. Easy roads prove hazardous. Expectations prove ephemeral. Control is an illusion.

We will find our way by finding our way. We will pay our taxes to the emperor, as it were, and then learn to see the coin's holier context. It will always be a struggle and leave us bruised.

But if there be anger and sadness, let there be anger and sadness. If there be confusion and angst, let there be confusion and angst. Life isn't a neat package. Life will be found by daring to see. My mother didn't call yesterday to wish me Happy Birthday. She lies in a hospital bed and cannot speak. But she gave me birth, my father faithfully at hand, and now it is my turn to remember.

Story

Mark 1:23-24: Just then there was in their synagogue a man with an unclean spirit, and he cried out, "What have you to do with us, Jesus of Nazareth? Have you come to destroy us? I know who you are, the Holy One of God."

If I could say one thing to the clergy and spouses whom I will lead on retreat this weekend in New England, what would it be? "Hang in there."

Hang in there with each other and with your own best selves. As the wild man recognized the instant he saw Jesus, ministry, done right, intrudes and disrupts the lives of the faithful. To them it can feel dangerous. And so they fight back, deploying two potent weapons: fear and trivialization.

Fear can corrode a household. Clergy marriages are notoriously unsettled. Being made to feel small can corrode self-confidence. Clergy are notoriously self-destructive. You need each other, and you need to remember your true self. People project all manner of feelings and self-loathing onto their clergy, but that isn't you.

Hang in there with your people. As a wise colleague, now a bishop, once remarked, "Church is the one place where the competent can get away with being incompetent." Hard-chargers in business can lapse into the slacker role. The ultra-responsible can behave like children. People who manage billions with aplomb can dither over thousands.

Church, in other words, is an escape in more ways than one. But see the hunger and neediness that lie within the inexplicable behavior. We are all running from ourselves. In full flight, we do things to each other that don't reflect our best.

Hang in there with your bishop or leader. If bishops and other judicatory executives aren't troubled, anxious, conflicted, and hesitant leaders, then they haven't been paying attention. If your

24

bishop strolls down the aisle with head held high and not an apparent care in the world, then he or she hasn't spent enough time in your homes and studies. Draw them closer.

Hang in there with the church. I personally am not convinced that the church, as we know it, is what God had in mind. Jesus had little regard for hierarchies, rules, standard procedures, or boundaries. It seems unlikely that he intended to launch an institution grounded in hierarchy, rule, procedure, and boundary. More likely, he intended a circle of friends, a household like your own households, gatherings of the weary and needy, pilgrims yearning for companionship on a tough journey.

> *If you can become a beacon for friendship and community, your flock can rise above institution and behave like people. Messy, but noble.*

If you can become a beacon for friendship and community, your flock can rise above institution and behave like people. Messy, but noble.

Hang in there with God. Your Savior has come to transform you, to lead you home. It isn't about safety, comfort, complete knowledge, clear or clever ideas, or tidy rituals fussed over. It isn't about power or privilege or any of the other frauds perpetrated in God's name.

It is about hearts and hands, wounded souls and lives yearning to be free. It is about justice—not this or that political theory, but actual fairness and compassion. It is about a living Word—not right opinion bolstered by stray scriptures, but a Word that burrows inside and brings light to the darkness.

And hang in there with your own story. There is nothing more powerful than a personal story told truly. A true story can transform. It is the only bridge to other people's stories. Theories, doctrines, and pronouncements are like noise. A true story is like manna in the desert.

The bravest preacher is the one who says, "This is my story, this is how I hear God's story, and now tell me your story." If the demons that press down upon us are to be unseated, then a true and godly story needs to take root. In the end, your story is all that you have to tell.

Family
and
Community

⚬

Love of family takes patience, forbearance, forgiveness,

and compassion—and therefore is a model for

understanding God. Jesus formed circles rather than

hierarchies. Jesus embraced rather than excluded. Until we

set aside our hierarchies of power and our determination to

create outcasts, we will have little to say to a needy world.

Partners

Matthew 18:22: Jesus said to him, "Not seven times, but, I tell you, seventy-seven times."

On the eve of a Day of Remembrance—perhaps also a Day of Renewed Terror—my eleven-year-old son and I do normal things, and they are good.

First, we go to the polls to vote. At a time when flags will be waving, bells ringing, and school assemblies singing patriotic songs, I want him to see what makes our nation work. I explain political parties, primary elections, precincts, ballots. I point to the voting booth. "This is the heart of it," I say, "a free and private ballot. I can hold whatever opinions I want, I can speak my mind, I can vote for whomever I choose, and no one stands over my shoulder."

Then off to the mall to shop for his first dress-up clothes. Dancing school starts Friday. He walks in wearing a well-traveled T-shirt, soccer shorts, and sneakers. Soon, he stands before me in a blue blazer, khakis, and white dress shirt, a handsome young man ready for the next adventure.

I suspect the manners they teach in Junior Cotillion will be a bit starchy. But I want two things for my son. I want him to learn the joy of dancing—the wild and wonderful freedom that comes from waltzing around a room, turning patterns into flight. Even more, I want him to treat girls with dignity and respect. Girls are different from boys, never more so than when adolescence beckons, but girls aren't the enemy, they aren't objects, they don't exist for his pleasure. Girls have their own identities. They can say "no" when asked to dance, or they can say "yes." Girls can be partners in the swooshing waltz of life, but he cannot demand that partnership, only request it.

If the terrorists who wait for another signal to strike truly understood what makes us tick, and what makes us threatening to them, they wouldn't attack office buildings or airports. They would have to go from town to town and find all of the gyms and parish halls where free citizens cast free ballots. Yes, we might exit the polls and some turn right and some turn left, some to elegant homes and some to shabby, some to privilege and some to deprivation. But we each have one vote—every one of us, not just landowners, fair-skinned, or religiously correct—and as officeholders discover to their surprise, you cannot ignore citizens for long.

> Girls aren't the enemy, they aren't objects.

A black man will stand up in public and declare that his dreams count, too, and some day—maybe not soon enough but some day—his dreams will be heard. The rich and powerful might seem to have their way in all things, but as many are discovering now, they aren't exempt from the laws. Or any likelier to be content or to die in peace.

The terror-minded would have to go to dancing schools, family kitchens, bedtime talks, schools, churches—all of those places where we are trying to escape humankind's long and tragic history of oppressing women. While they treat women as property, with no rights, no voices, and no faces, we are trying to see each other as God sees us.

We have a long way to go. I doubt that Cotillion's requirement of white gloves for girls will constitute a step forward. But my son will stand before his partner in the dance, and he will see a person.

They can attack our buildings, our public assemblies, our water supplies, the air we breathe, and the Internet on which we depend, but they cannot close down our voting booths, and whether our sons and daughters are dancing or learning to bear arms, they will be partners, as persons, as equals, as children of God, each deserving dignity and respect.

We will not go back to former days.

Commencement

John 15:9: [Jesus said] "As the Father has loved me, so I have loved you; abide in my love."

R ain threatens but restrains itself throughout the two-hour commencement ceremony in the University of North Carolina football stadium. It takes us a while to locate our twenty-two-year-old son in the sea of Carolina blue filling end-zone seats. But once we do, events on stage at the 50-yard line make more sense, especially comedian Bill Cosby's stunning address.

Once awarded his honorary degree and introduced as speaker, Cosby sheds his academic gown and strides forward wearing a Carolina sweatshirt and a UNC baseball cap festooned with tassel. The crowd roars.

As only a great and beloved comedian can do, Cosby speaks with mock sternness to the graduates. "It's over!" he tells them. The cushy life isolated from adult responsibilities, viewing home as a laundry service, skating by with shopworn excuses—"It's all over!" Now "you are one of us," he cackles. "Ha, ha."

If any other grownup said this, it would sound harsh. But Cosby's affection is manifest. He makes it okay to ask the question that graduates are asking in this unsettling age, "Now what?"

He motions to families seated in the stands. "They love you," he says. Picking up the same theme, the senior class president says to the graduates, "On the count of three, say, 'Thanks, Mom! Thanks, Dad!'" He makes the count, and a roar of thanks arises from the blue sea. My heart catches.

Afterward, rain starts in earnest, forcing us to move our between-ceremonies picnic indoors. But we are proud and dry when our son receives his diploma in the Computer Science department's afternoon ceremony.

As we head back to our car for champagne, I walk behind our three sons and marvel at who they are becoming, as individuals and as brothers.

I cannot trace our ups and downs in this unsettling age. I know that we have endured more than some and far less than others. But I know that I am proud of our graduate and his accomplishments, and I am grateful for the paired blessings of clouds and sunlight.

In saying farewell to his friends, Jesus said they would "abide" in his love. Life would separate their courses, but they would remain in each other. Whatever began in their brief time together would continue to join them, changed but steadfast.

Jesus knew their fears. He knew his talk of departure was disturbing. Like these graduates, they wondered how goodbye could mean hello, how completion could be called "commencement," how an end could constitute a beginning. They would find out only by venturing forth.

> *Like a parent to a child, sometimes God walks ahead of us, showing us the way. Sometimes beside us, listening and comforting. Sometimes behind us, marveling at who we are becoming.*

"It's rough out there," Cosby told the nervous. Indeed it is. Not enough jobs, not enough peace, a political world spinning wildly, too many looters, too many predators, too much fraud, plus the self-doubts that seize every child commencing to adulthood.

Cosby didn't use the biblical word "abide," but I think that is what he meant as he gestured to families in the stands and to graduates in the end zone and tried with his gift of humor to underscore our oneness. Whatever lies ahead in this unsettling age, we have each other. Abide in that.

Like a parent to a child, sometimes God walks ahead of us, showing us the way. Sometimes beside us, listening and comforting. Sometimes behind us, marveling at who we are becoming. Like the comedian urging end zone and sidelines to look at each other, not at him, Jesus urged us to turn our heads and to look for God.

We must share umbrellas, move some picnics indoors, say good-bye even as we negotiate hello, sense each other's joys, fears, and sorrows, and every once in a while dare to shout our gratitude.

"That came off pretty well, didn't it?" says our son about the unison cascade of thanks. Yes, it did.

Home

Mark 1:29: As soon as they left the synagogue, they entered the house of Simon and Andrew, with James and John.

On my way home from leading a clergy/spouse retreat in the White Mountains, my wife and I spend a night in the southern New Hampshire town where her family has lived for two centuries. I have known this town for twenty-six years, longer than I have known anywhere except the city of my birth.

I have sat in this kitchen overlooking fields and woodlands from the days I was courting their daughter through the growing-up of our sons, and now to the final days before my father-in-law moves to a retirement center. In this chair I have fretted and fussed, glowed and laughed, guided my children, planned for tomorrow, revised my plans, written hundreds of meditations, read countless newspapers and vacation novels, watched my mother-in-law's chair go empty, and heard extended-family stories change from diapers to colleges.

It seems unreal to think that we will never sit this way again. Unreal to think that "home" is such a movable feast, even in rural New England where longevity is measured in centuries. Unreal to think that someone else—a good family, thank goodness, a farmer and his pregnant wife—will be making their home here in three months.

I look at kitchen counters laden with stuff—some of it stuff that hasn't moved in twenty years—and see, not a cooking area reduced to two square feet, but a family's way of being at home. I look at a wall covered with snapshots, of a family in full extension. I look at my wife sitting across the table and cannot fully imagine what this moment means to her.

It is no small matter to leave home. No matter how many times we do it, it hurts to pack up furnishings and memories and take them to new places. It confuses to stand up from a table as if it were no more than, say, a diner. Where will we gather next time?

We will gather, of course, for family remains family, even as generations transition and die, even as nephews go to sea, even as new loves create new households. As long as someone remembers this kitchen—not the space of course, but the heartbeat—we will be connected.

When Jesus began to form his circle of friendship—which we must stop seeing as an institution, a hierarchy-in-formation, a mustering of "superheroes," a designating of categories of what is acceptable before God, but a circle of men and women whom Jesus called "friends"—he began by leading them away from home. For home can be a snare, a prison, a bastion against the very thing that God desires, namely, newness of life. Home can set artificial boundaries on dreams and daring, and enshrine familiarity above all else.

But then Jesus led them back home. They were becoming different, and he was in their midst. But, as I read the story, Jesus wanted them to know that newness of life doesn't wage war on family or home, but rather newness of life transforms. Now Simon could love his family in a new way. Now Simon could bring new hope to the vagaries of life.

> The measure of home isn't stability of place, it is our capacity, through the grace of God, to love each other in ever-new ways.

Just as the family centered in this New Hampshire kitchen has been transformed by newness of life, so will the homes of God's people everywhere be transformed. Yes, God calls us all onto the road, out into the world, into a journey of repentance and sacrifice. But the measure of home isn't stability of place, it is our capacity, through the grace of God, to love each other in ever-new ways.

In the end, home is the circle, not the property.

Choose

John 15:16: [Jesus said] "You did not choose me but I chose you. And I appointed you to go and bear fruit, fruit that will last."

How was graduation?" asks the woman behind the cheese counter. I bought Prima Donna and Gouda from her a week ago for our picnic at commencement. She recognizes me and remembers.

In a city that is large enough to be anonymous, being recognized means a lot. That's why I shop here, rather than up the street.

Same with the day's banking. I am switching from one bank to another. The former has better ads and a spectacular new logo. But I never stopped being a stranger. So why put up with high fees? At my new bank, a friendly teller looks me in the eye and smiles. I'll take that over ads and logo any day.

Same with list-service providers. I recently changed services. I could tolerate the former's inconsistent service if customer support were anything more than an automated reply center with no human contact. At my new provider, I call for support and spend ten minutes talking to the firm's president.

Same with churches. We all want different things from the faith community. Speaking for myself, what I want is to be recognized. I want to be known by name and treasured as a person. Not a name on a list, not one more duty for the pastor, but a whole person, embraced and encouraged.

Why does recognition matter? It's more than ego needs. It's more than finding some antidote to anonymity. It has to do with mutuality of choosing.

I choose where to shop, bank, and worship. Freedom of choice is a core value in this land. But choice by itself can be a bleak exercise if there isn't some choosing in return.

My former bank, for example, tries in its ads to convince me that I am smart and elite to choose them. Most ads are like that nowadays, selling image rather than service, derivative status rather than recognition. But that is nonsense. A bank is a bank is a bank. My new bank, klutzy non-status place that it is, chooses to serve its customers, not to sell them on accepting non-service.

That's the mutuality of choosing. I can choose one cheese shop over another, but for anything meaningful to occur, the cheese clerk has to choose me.

That's the miracle of romance: not that one chose the perfect partner, but that the choosing was mutual. Two people who are trying to connect can overcome all manner of adversity and inadequacy. But if one partner is all take and no give, then good fortune, good looks, and good technique count for nothing.

Jesus wanted his disciples to know that he had chosen them. They weren't losers who had nothing else to do, or broken souls who had no other escape route, or sinners whose stain was so dark that no one else would receive them. They were a treasure, chosen freely.

> *Jesus looked them in the eye and smiled with delight.*

Christians have wanted to hear Jesus' words as conferring elite status and raising them above all possibility of error. But that wasn't his point. He chose them, they chose him; he knew them by name, they knew him. They were in him, and he was in them. This wasn't about receiving a "free pass" to heaven, as if one could choose the perfect path, like the perfect bank, and win the prize. Jesus looked them in the eye and smiled with delight.

That is what made them such a potent force in the world: not infallibility, not right opinion, not intellectual or spiritual superiority, and certainly not good techniques, handsome image bearers, tall steeples, and fine Web sites. They changed the world by being loved first, known by name, chosen freely, and sent forth as servants with capability.

Submit

John 15:13: [Jesus said] "No one has greater love than this, to lay down one's life for one's friends."

Yet another day of rain reminds me of a concert I attended in Tipton, Indiana, in the heart of corn country. A sold-out house became unexpectedly sparse. In the distance, competing with the symphony, we heard the rumble of John Deeres. After a wet spring, "the men can finally get in the fields," said a neighbor. Plant now, or lose a season.

In my case, rain stalls the pouring of a driveway at our new house. I can hear the builder announcing another delay in closing. Shall I fuss or threaten reprisal? Shall I remind the builder of his original schedule? What's the point? It's like analyzing an accident and then blaming someone for wrong place, wrong time. Second-guessing feels good, but contributes nothing.

No more helpful is the gloating comment, "I knew this would happen." I remember a colleague who received any report with a superior nod, to indicate that he had known all along, and why was I so slow?

Better, I think, to look reality in the eye and to make choices grounded in wisdom. Sometimes the wise course is to submit to reality. Accept aging, for example, or give up a concert ticket because planting takes priority.

Sometimes the wise course is to resist. Kids face this choice every day, as soft drink and tobacco manufacturers try to establish an air of inevitability about using their products. How many would-be dieters have stood at a buffet line and shrugged, "What can I do?"

Sometimes we need to change course, sometimes we need to stand firm. Neither accommodation nor rigidity is inherently virtuous.

Jesus knew that hard choices lay ahead for his disciples. His ministry had challenged the established order. The custodians of tradition would fight back.

Some waged open war on believers, sending zealots like Saul of Tarsus to hunt them down. Some labeled them "blasphemers," drunkards, and crazy. Some resistance was internal, as pride and greed stirred sectarian conflict. Men drove women out of the inner circle. Rome's bishop trounced all others. Monarchs, dictators, and social elites co-opted the church with blandishments, money, and exclusion.

The choices posed by faith are never easy. They can't be reduced to a buying opportunity—this Bible translation or that, this denomination or that—for those are trivial diversions. Nor can faith's choices be declared already settled, as if inherited tradition said it all. Knotty issues simply cannot be resolved by prowling Leviticus.

Reality changes, and so does God. Scripture reveals a God who submits to reality—not because God caused Adam and Eve to sin and hide, but because once they did, the garden's reality had changed and God had to abandon that dream. The victory over Canaan turned sour, so God changed course. Don't build a temple, God told David. Okay, build a temple, God told Solomon. Life with God is a dialogue, not a monologue.

> *Life with God is a dialogue, not a monologue.*

What, then, is our measure? That is the haunting question. If ethics are situational, if God's will is found in movement, not on a rock that never stirs, if truth emerges in wilderness, how can we make wise and faithful choices?

The commandment, said Jesus, is to "love one another." And that means this: "lay down your lives for each other." Submit to each other, sacrifice for the other, be willing to listen and to lose, put the other's needs first, be servants and friends, not rulers and enemies.

Some day we will step back from the buffet line, and instead of asking chicken or beef, we will ask, "Where is my neighbor? Where is the child who has no food?" Reality isn't limited to the choice I wish to make, but goes much deeper, to that level where love means sacrifice.

Orphaned

John 14:18: [Jesus said] "I will not leave you orphaned; I am coming to you."

She looks eight months pregnant, a teenager, and alone. As the serving line moves forward at the Homeless Shelter, she tries to join a nearby conversation. She is white, they are black, and they don't quite connect. But she seems to relax just having someone to stand next to.

Her eager face and protruding belly tell a story beyond knowing.

She is someone's daughter, but whoever bore her couldn't protect her into adulthood. While luckier girls were primping for proms and deciding among colleges, she was elsewhere.

She is someone's lover. One night, many nights, who knows? But he is gone, and she is left alone, carrying a baby whom she has little wherewithal to raise. She will try. She might get lucky.

She will soon be a mother. A statistic, too: another unwed teenage mother, another drain on state medical funds, another occasion for moralizing by those who fight abortion, free birth control, and welfare and then condemn those who need them.

But, still, a mother, the comforter and life support of a child, the one who can make a difference between loved and unloved, between fed and unfed, between safe and unsafe. Her child's future will be shaped by the nutrition and care that she is able to offer. What will be in her breast milk? What will she feed an infant at the time when his or her brain is growing exponentially? What spirit will she instill?

Tonight, as usual on Homeless Shelter nights, we stop at Boston Market, a restaurant, for our own dinner. It always feels fitting to eat at this particular place. For this restaurant seems to specialize in people who are just barely making it. Weary single moms muster the

40

energy to engage their children in dinner-table conversation. Solitary men work on the day's sales reports. It is almost bleak some nights.

The food is great, which is why we come. But I also sense that we need to see something here: the line between making it and not making it is narrow and blurry. Large outcomes start with a lucky break here, a bad break there, a fling that didn't yield conception, a fling that did, a partner who is steadfast, a partner who is weak, and those unavoidable facts of life: skin color and gender.

When you serve food to those who have no food and imagine story lines for those whose future is daunting, there is little energy left for judgment or moralizing. There is room only for sadness. And that, I believe, is exactly the point at which the Spirit of God comes to us.

Jesus never debated social policy. He never asked whether a hungry person deserved food. He refused to judge the woman caught in adultery. When his disciples tried to defend themselves against a confusing situation by asking who had sinned, Jesus simply cared. Jesus never traded votes, never used the needy as pawns to sell phony slogans like "Leave No Child Behind." Jesus never stood in a homeless shelter and dispassionately sorted people into categories for reports that no one will read. Jesus gave food, healing, presence, fellow servants, and ultimately his life.

> *We cannot expand the suburbs far enough. Misfortune and mortality will find us all. And so, we hope, will God.*

"I will not leave you orphaned," he promised. I take that to mean something tangible: the Spirit will see the eager face of a frightened girl and care for her. I don't know how, but I know that we are all betting our futures on a God who sees the sadness, who sees the thin and blurry line of making it, who sees the weary mother and the lonely man.

We try to live far away from homeless shelters and bleak restaurants. But we cannot expand the suburbs far enough. Misfortune and mortality will find us all. And so, we hope, will God.

Servants

Mark 2:3-4: Some people came, bringing to [Jesus] a paralyzed man, carried by four of them. And when they could not bring him to Jesus because of the crowd, they removed the roof above him; and after having dug through it, they let down the mat on which the paralytic lay.

After watching it for the seventh time, I conclude that *Gosford Park*, directed by Robert Altman, is my candidate for best film ever.

Some would name others. The American Film Institute, for example, names *Citizen Kane*, followed by *Casablanca*, *The Godfather*, *Gone with the Wind*, and *Lawrence of Arabia*. But as film critics could teach religious warriors, opinions don't constitute objective truth.

Gosford Park operates on one level as a murder mystery, on another as a comedy of manners, and then has several layers still to go, each one a commentary on the human condition. The film seems perfectly cast, with established stars like Maggie Smith and Kristin Scott Thomas mumbling deliciously as useless upper-class snobs, and lesser-knowns displaying depth as the below-stairs servants.

The cinematography shows Altman at his finest. In precisely framed and yet free-flowing tracking shots, characters are preceded by their sounds and are sketched in by brief interactions, the way life works. Scenes are more like ballet than the usual two people talking or fighting.

Above stairs, a dozen stories circle around a hateful war profiteer who now (1932) lords it over everyone. He is the centerpiece below stairs, too, not only because, as one maid says, servants' lives are only a reflection of their masters, but because he has actively abused them, as well.

In imagining four men carrying a paralyzed friend to Jesus, I think of the "upstairs/downstairs" clash at Gosford Park. Upstairs, insecure snobs prey on one another. One cad gets a young girl pregnant, and another cad blackmails her. Two sisters cut cards to see who marries the lecherous magnate. The one decent person is sneered at for not having a personal maid and for bringing only one evening gown. A film star is reduced to providing entertainment at the piano.

Stories are more vivid and passions more genuine "downstairs." At table, they sit by rank (a countess's servant ranks above a baroness's), but in the end they work hard together and treat each other decently. When the housekeeper says, "I am the perfect servant, and that means I don't have a life," Altman leaves the viewer to nod in sad comprehension, but then to say, "No, you have far more life than those helpless fools upstairs, who know nothing more than etiquette."

As I try to picture four men carrying a friend, I see Altman's below-stairs servants supporting one another. Not predators scoring on another's weakness, not blustery attitudes demanding attention, not snobs insisting that, by any proper pecking order, the crowd should part for them, not whiners like the countess

> *Faith cuts holes—in roofs, in pompous egos, in moneyed barriers.*

who cannot even open a thermos bottle for herself. I see guys caring for a friend.

Jesus called his disciples "servants" and "friends." In a class-divided world, he placed them below stairs, where burdens are high, rewards are few, reflected status feels empty, and the powerful get their way. Few people would choose that world, for it always seems prettier to dress for dinner and to be waited on. In many hands, religion becomes a tool for enhancing status.

But faith points to servanthood, not mastery. Faith knows power as addictive, not exemplary. Faith knows vulnerability as inviting embrace, not exploitation. Faith knows snobbery as empty-headed. Faith knows privilege as cruel. Faith sees authenticity, not reflected glory.

Faith cuts holes—in roofs, in pompous egos, in moneyed barriers.

Altman labels *Gosford Park*, circa 1932, as sad, gone, and not much lamented. For him, hope lies in the plucky servant who is punished for speaking freely and then breaks free from such a stifling world.

Fear

Mark 5:35-36: Some people came from the leader's house to say, "Your daughter is dead. Why trouble the teacher any further?" But overhearing what they said, Jesus said to the leader of the synagogue, "Do not fear, only believe."

Some fears are groundless—worthy of being taken seriously, just not grounded in reality. When my son left for Boy Scout camp, for example, he was anxious—filled with nameless dread. The absence of calls suggests that safe and pleasing reality has overcome his fears.

Some fears are based on facts not yet known, like the contents of a letter not yet opened, the outcome of a vote not yet taken, or a physician's report not yet issued.

Some fears, however, are well grounded and well documented. There is nothing more to discover. The vote is announced—you lost. The report is made—cancer. Now cascade fear of the fact known, fear of the next consequence not yet known, and nameless dread.

In this swirl of fears, faith has a hard time gaining a foothold. Should faith spiritualize the situation and say that none of this is real, only God is real, and God has "something better in mind"?

Should faith challenge the facts, demanding that God modify reality to make it more acceptable? Change the vote, make the cancer go away.

Or does faith offer, not a way out of reality, but a way in? Not a better result, but a better heart for facing the result? In other words, is God that large, omnipotent grownup who does whatever it takes to make the child's world safe? Or is God a companion who shares the load in love, like a partner who stands with you before the child's coffin and joins your weeping?

In *The New Yorker* I read a powerful poem called "The Clerk's Tale," by Spencer Reece. Two clerks at a Minnesota mall tell the "muscled, groomed and cropped" about fashions, while they engage in their own pretense until it is time to leave. In their separate cars they loosen their ties. "We are alone. There is no longer any need to express ourselves."

Bleak, insightful, a searing tale of modern anonymity. Imagine God entering this bleakness. To encourage more pretense—these long and empty hours are nothing compared to the "great bye and bye"? No, God isn't into pretense. To join in resenting the money counters who leave them feeling "older, dirtier, dwarfed"? No, God isn't our partisan against the other.

Imagine God sitting beside the clerk in his car, assuring him that he isn't alone or without value. Peddling foulards to strangers isn't all that life could have been. But here I am, says God, still loving you, still believing in you, still wanting to sit beside you. What would we not give for such a companion!

> *Here I am, says God, still loving you, still believing in you, still wanting to sit beside you.*

When the religious leader Jairus approached Jesus, he wanted the Master to change reality. Make the illness go away. But then came people bearing facts: your daughter is dead. When Jesus told him, "Do not fear, only believe," what was he offering Jairus?

Jesus knew the girl was asleep, not dead. He might have been offering Jairus better information. But what happens when there is no better information? The war continues, the loved one dies, and that is that. Has Jesus not cared?

I think Jesus was offering companionship. Let us walk into death together. Let us open the envelope together, sit at the doctor's desk together, face reality together. If reality proves different from what you expect, then we will rejoice together. If reality remains as feared, then we will hold each other.

Either way, you aren't "alone."

Corner

John 1:51: [Jesus said to Nathanael] "Very truly, I tell you, you will see heaven opened and the angels of God ascending and desceding upon the Son of Man."

My father and I walk down to the corner. He uses two canes nowadays but is determined to stay mobile, even on an icy winter day in Indianapolis.

A leftover from the days when small shops congregated every few blocks at trolley stops, 49th and Penn remains lively. Some shops are longtime stalwarts—pharmacy, dry cleaner, market— and some are new, like the two coffee shops, bank, hardware store, and art gallery.

Gone are the little shack where I paid my newspaper delivery bill, and the stores where I spent my profits: a lunch counter, Lindner's ice-cream shop, and Tune Spot record store. Gone is the fish market where a Jewish survivor of Nazi Germany made a fresh start. The corner is down to one gas station from three.

Long gone is the trolley, which I used to board at 52nd Street and ride down to 33rd for boys' choir rehearsals, my first venture into urban independence. Now Pennsylvania features buses, joggers in high-tech gear, and automobiles.

If an urban planner were given this area to build from scratch, I doubt that he would create this. The housing mix is too uneven, making it difficult for homeowners to predict who their neighbors will be. The shops aren't glossy or the parking adequate.

But cities evolve. They aren't created whole cloth. When a community is created on a drawing board, rather than in decades of good and bad decisions, the results tend to be lifeless and precious.

This corner of 49th and Penn is quirky. But communities need quirks and odd vistas. They need familiar faces and new faces, even strange faces. They need people who walk, who talk as they walk, who savor life as something to be enjoyed.

Communities don't need to be frozen in anyone's memory, for fighting change is a death sentence to any community. But they do need memories and an awareness that we build on something. The art gallery owner says he loved knowing that the long groove in his cement floor was once used for washing away fish debris, even as the fishmonger washed away the evil stench of the Holocaust.

When God decided to try again, to re-create, to restore what had been lost, he didn't return to the drawing board, as if the millennia hadn't happened. God planted a new vine in an old vineyard, and then nurtured that vine, so that life could flourish.

Jesus told Nathanael that he would see angels ascending and descending upon the Son of Man. One could rhapsodize about the sight of angels, but I think his point was that God would nourish the vine. Into the blood-soaked soil of proud Israel, God would plant a Messiah, a new glimpse of grace.

> Into the blood-soaked soil of proud Israel, God would plant a Messiah, a new glimpse of grace.

He would empower that Messiah with heart and soul to call humanity back to its senses.

God did that powerfully for a brief period, as Jesus ministered to the poor and needy, offended the wealthy and smug, and showed a face of God that the religious establishment had denied.

But what about today? I believe that the vine did flourish, and still flourishes, occasionally in the institutions that claim Messiah's mantle, but more often in the lives of people who are willing to dare what Jesus dared. Like an urban landscape, who they are and what they do tends to evolve, as needs and personalities change.

That restless evolution often bothers the institutions that thought themselves entitled to eternal tenancy on prominent street corners. But if life is to flow through Messiah's vine, the angels of God need freedom to shout and to whisper, to encourage and to chastise, to protect the weak and dreamy from being squashed by the powerful, to breathe new life.

Respect

Matthew 23:6-7: Jesus said, "They [the scribes and Pharisees] love to have the place of honor at banquets and the best seats in the synagogues, and to be greeted with respect in the marketplaces, and to have people call them rabbi."

I watch my eleven-year-old son finish a session of Junior Cotillion. He listens attentively, hands more or less on his knees, as instructed. He stands and offers his arm to the girl next to him. She slips a white-gloved left hand lightly onto his arm, as instructed, and they walk to the door, looking self-conscious but content. Each sneaks a glance at the other, to make sure they are doing this right.

On our drive home, he tells me about learning the cha-cha and how to help a girl into a limousine. Neither skill is likely to be required often in his life, but beneath the specifics of manners is an important lesson: show respect.

In learning the right way to escort a girl, a boy learns small ways to show her respect. He gets outside himself and becomes attentive.

The girl, in turn, allows herself to be escorted, a waiting-to-be-asked that she might later want to question. But the point isn't who leads whom. The point is the transaction of respect, in which each attends to the other. Perhaps Cotillion ways will seem stilted, but I hope the lesson will remain: respect is given, not demanded.

One of the greatest gifts that parents give children is respect. When I teach my son's elementary school class one hour a week, I can tell which kids are shown respect at home and which aren't. The former, believing themselves worthy of respect, ask questions and speak with a confidence that says, *My words matter*. Those not shown respect at home either slouch away or wave their hands violently, as if the only way to get attention is to make a scene.

Later in life, partners give this gift of respect to each other. In Cotillion, partnerships are admittedly contrived. But every child is being taught. You are worthy of respect. You don't need to be manipulative or demanding. You can offer your hand to another and know that you are worthy of being treated well. If you get "dissed," it won't be because you deserved it.

Marriages and partnerships would be so much richer if partners believed themselves worthy of respect. So would workplaces. So would neighborhoods. So would cities. I hear many people yearning for community and wondering how we could rethink structures and power allocations to bring community about. The heart of community isn't structure or power, it is respect.

> The heart of community isn't structure or power, it is respect.

Jesus condemned the religious establishment of his day because they demanded respect but showed no respect in return. They seized places of honor, and insisted on greetings and titles. But they looked down on others and criticized Jesus for consorting with the lowly. With a disdain for others that director Robert Altman captures perfectly in the film *Gosford Park,* the religious leaders were like "whitewashed tombs," said Jesus, looking righteous but filled with "bones" and "filth."

His words against the scribes and Pharisees were harsh, as were those of John the Baptist. Their sin wasn't inadequate doctrine or wrong opinion. Their sin was violating the transaction of respect. They were like the super-rich who turn governments, tax laws, stock markets, and corporate practices to their self-serving ends and show no respect for those who actually do the work from which they benefit or who suffer at their selfish hands.

They were like the ultra-pious who judge others but think themselves beyond questioning. They were like the politicians who manipulate elections and smear opponents, take their tainted victories as "mandates" from the people, and proceed to distance themselves from the unwashed.

Respect, you see, goes way beyond manners. Respect—love in action—is the cement of civilization.

Margins

Mark 1:27: "They were all amazed, and they kept on asking one another, "What is this? A new teaching—with authority! He commands even the unclean spirits and they obey him."

What do you think a 'church on the margins' would look like?" asks a pastor after my second talk at this retreat for clergy and partners.

Clergy are rarely consulted on public policy, except as window dressing for opinion-shapers. Election-year "prayer breakfasts" are photo ops for politicians, not occasions for probing the mind of God. Conservative evangelicals are in fashion nowadays, but they will find their spotlight brief. Their mega-pastors, like Roman prelates and Presbyterian preachers before them, will discover they are tools for the powerful, and the tool must conform to the hand that wields it, or it will be discarded.

Many older towns assumed that churches and synagogues would occupy important real estate. But newer communities are centered on commerce, not steeples. Church festivals no longer shape public life.

Rather than view life "on the margins" as a sign of decline, we should know that the margins are where we should have been all along. For that is where Jesus served, and two millennia of efforts to occupy center stage, to be kingmakers and princes, yielded more warfare than peace, more arrogance than tolerance.

As conservative evangelicals are demonstrating now in their brief turn on stage, Christians tend to turn mean and ugly when we are given the reins. Our tendency toward absolutes and certainty renders us unfit for worldly power. We will compromise too much in pursuit of wealth and victory.

So, asks a pastor, what would a "church on the margins" look like?

It would be noisy and chaotic. It would be servant, not master. It would embrace all kinds and offer bread to any uplifted hand. It would love the unlovable and learn from the weak. It would listen to cries of pain and share God's outrage when one person imposes suffering on another. It would be "radical," as Jesus was radical, namely, getting to the root of things and not being swayed by the superficial.

A church on the margins would be poor in coin but rich in compassion. It would see oppression at every level, including the tendency of worldly power to oppress even those who think themselves masters. It would dare to question and to disturb, knowing that good news always stands in contrast to bad news.

A church on the margins would look beyond its own prejudices and categories, its own doctrines and certainties, and would try to imagine God's fresh word for a confusing dawn. It would reexamine everything—and I mean everything—in its hunger to see the face of Jesus. For our one foundation is nothing we or our ancestors ever built.

> *"What do you think a 'church on the margins' would look like?"*

A church on the margins would be a circle of friends—a disorderly circle, and an odd assortment of friends. It would be grounded in listening, not oratory; in discovery, not catechism; in catching the tunes of human hearts, not arguing over appropriate music. It would set aside all privilege, even the much-prized prerogatives awarded to clergy.

All voices would be valued, even those whom the world has dismissed as irrelevant, untutored, sinful, and worthless. All questions would be honored, all yearnings taken seriously. Not only would the wolf lie down with the lamb, but the lawyer would listen to the bricklayer, the scholar would learn from the homeless, and the world's carefully cultivated tastes and barriers would crumble to dust.

Then, and only then, would we be doing what Jesus did. Then would we know what happens when servants of God dare to shine light on the margins. Then would the darkness fight back, not co-opting us for photo-op prayers, but tasting its own uncleanness. Then would we be in trouble—but what glorious trouble to be in!

Message

Mark 1:28: At once [Jesus'] fame began to spread throughout the surrounding region of Galilee.

Surrounded by snow and the White Mountains in New Hampshire, in an isolated region where my cell phone finds no signal and Internet access proceeds at glacial speed, we gather for worship in a resort inn.

We are proceeding normally, when someone whispers to the celebrant, and suddenly the mood turns somber. He announces that the space shuttle apparently has disintegrated. With an intensity that I don't understand, he invites prayer.

Yes, this is a tragedy, but the daily news is filled with tragedies. Why does this one touch so deeply?

Later, as our host drives us from North Conway to my father-in-law's farm in southern New Hampshire, we pass by Concord High School. He says this was where Christa McAuliffe was teaching when she was chosen to be the first teacher-astronaut. Her shuttle exploded on takeoff. Even today, eighteen years later, apples and fresh flowers still appear regularly on her grave.

Now I understand this morning's intensity. It wasn't just a news flash that technology enabled CNN to disseminate speedily. It was the message itself. And not just the message, but how the message touched their lives.

Something similar is happening in other places. Television and newspaper reports show mourners gathering in places like Wisconsin. They suggest links between this tragedy and the terrorist attacks of September 2001—not that terrorists brought down the shuttle, but that huge and inexplicable loss touches a deep chord, perhaps a chord of newfound vulnerability.

I remember feeling a similar intensity when I covered my first coalmine explosion for the *Wall Street Journal,* and I witnessed the extraordinary grace of some miners, families, and townsfolk, and the boorishness of the operators who casually allowed these explosions to occur. I was an outsider, but I was touched by agony and injustice.

When news of Jesus spread rapidly around the Galilean countryside, it wasn't just a hyperactive "grapevine." It was the message—the kingdom of God had come near—and it was the way that message touched human hearts. News about Jesus found an eager ear, a fire ready to be kindled. When Jesus came to town, they brought their sick and needy to him. They brought their questions, their fears and self-loathing. He wasn't just a spectacle. He was a response to questions they were already asking, or if not asking, ready to ask if someone would just listen.

> When news of Jesus spread rapidly around the Galilean countryside, it wasn't just a hyperactive "grapevine."

Church leaders frequently ask, "What could we be doing better?" If we had the will to be effective and the courage to face the consequences, what would we be doing? Better planning? Better growth strategies? Better liturgy, better organizational management, better preparation of clergy, better training of laity? What?

It seems to me that life and God are already laying the fire. Hearts are troubled, brows are furrowed, minds are questioning, jobs are uncertain, finances are lean, our cities feel dangerous, injustice is epidemic, and now implacable enemies have us in their sights. We all ask different questions, but I think it is fair to say that few of us have found total serenity.

We are ready to hear good news. But someone has to listen to the stirrings of our hearts first. The message touches home because the "home" is ready to receive it. If faith communities would be effective, they need to listen first. If I could offer any prescription for church members, it would be to walk outside, to walk among the people, to listen and to be touched by everyday human tragedy.

This includes the usual parish prayer list, but it needs to go far beyond, to include needs that aren't yet converted to the comfortable cadence of prayer, and people who have no affiliation except our common humanity, and responses that cannot be confined to a tidy litany but allowed to resonate.

PART THREE

Control
Versus
Freedom

Control is both an illusion and an addiction. It is freedom that confers life and hope. Some want God to have a "plan." What God wants, it seems, is for us to make better choices.

Blame

Mark 4:41: [The disciples] were filled with great awe and said to one another, "Who then is this, that even the wind and the sea obey him?"

I receive my stopwatch, choose lane 3, and greet my fellow timer. We chat amiably until the swim meet begins. Then an odd pattern emerges. We each time the same swimmer. Our times sometimes differ by five or six hundredths of a second, sometimes by as much as three-tenths of a second. Amateur fingers on manual stopwatches are fallible.

Her response seems odd. When our times are close, she says, "Good, you're close." When the gap is wider, she administers a not-too-subtle silent treatment. She never doubts that her time is the accurate one.

A man walks over to chat, and she laces into him, accusing him of lying about some lapse in parenting. "Get your story straight," she says. When he walks away, she shakes her head in disgust. She refers to him as her ex-husband, "father of my child." Clearly, she blames him for all that undid their marriage, just as she blames me for different stopwatch readings. I consider bristling, but I realize this is one well-defended woman, and even entertaining the possibility of being wrong isn't within her grasp.

The divorce courts, of course, are replete with variants of this scenario. Nothing kills a relationship more thoroughly than blame. If partners cannot err, they cannot live. If partners cannot admit error, they cannot love.

Faith should have so much to say about blame. Scripture tells of a God who has mercy, who negotiates, who changes his mind, who repents of his own anger, who urges reconciliation, who is more concerned with loving enemies than demolishing them.

Faith is about discovery, not about defending expectations. Witness the difference between the disciples, who observed Jesus in action and asked, "Who is this?" and the religious establishment, who saw the same power but called him "blasphemer" for trespassing on their expectations.

But in practice, religion often ends up like this parched soul who defends herself with blaming. Religion has deemed itself the search for perfection—perfect laws, perfect practices, perfect beliefs, perfect leaders—and not what Jesus himself modeled, namely, the place where imperfection finds a home and failure finds forgiveness.

> *Faith is about discovery, not about defending expectations.*

Church councils at every level struggle with the question, *What if we get it wrong?* What if we misplace a comma in the creed? What if our reading of Genesis 1 is too literal? What if we encourage believers to think for themselves and they arrive at fresh conclusions? What if we change a long-standing practice? What if the altar isn't dressed perfectly or a crumb falls to the floor? What if the budget falls short or the new pastor has flaws?

Blamers are legion. They dominate our blame-ridden politics. They run many companies and sit on many church councils. They are the mother who blamed me for ruining her daughter's perfect wedding by calling attention to the groom's alcoholic rages. They are the senior warden who never accepted one iota of responsibility for the tension between us.

It would be so much better for us to be asking, "Who then are you?" I see your power, or your weakness, and I wonder who you are. I see you as different, and I wonder who you are. I hear you singing different songs, praying in different ways, seeking different assurances, asking different questions, measuring time in a different way, and I wonder who you are. If I knew you, then your being different wouldn't threaten me. But until I know you, the differences compel me to whatever form of self-defense and rage that I find safe.

Blame seeks the delusional safety of control. Faith asks the question—of God and of each other—"Who then are you?"

Customs

Mark 2:18: John's disciples and the Pharisees were fasting; and people came and said to [Jesus], "Why do John's disciples and the disciples of the Pharisees fast, but your disciples do not fast?"

My wife and I put on mud boots and walk up an unpaved driveway to our future home. At long last, active construction is under way. We walk through first-floor space that is framed but still open to the sky. We walk slowly from room to room, gauging room size, imagining doors and windows, imagining beyond studs and plywood, imagining a bed here, a sofa there.

We imagine living here in space we designed. We want the space to fit—and so far, every room looks right-sized for the way we live. But I also know that we will change, as new vistas, corners, and traffic patterns stir new ways of being indoors.

We have avoided exotic touches, partly with resale values in mind, mainly because we are relatively plain people. Even so, visitors will inevitably wonder why we made certain choices: a large dining room, for example, a study in the front corner, or an oversized screen porch.

The answer: this is who we are. We have certain values, and in building a house from scratch, we are given the opportunity to incarnate those values. The question isn't, why didn't we do what they would do, but rather, who are we, and what in us can be known by our choices?

Jesus had barely begun his ministry when the emerging habits of his household began to threaten people, because they strayed from customary patterns.

His inner circle, for example, included women as well as men, and sinners as well as the righteous. They moved about, rather than establish camps or structures, and they ventured among the unwashed. Their circle was open, rather than closed, and their center wasn't a flattering teacher or charismatic demagogue, but a moody man who ran from his own fame and spurned talk of thrones.

For example, why not require fasting? Why not observe the Sabbath according to tradition? If Jesus were just another ambitious leader vying for their favor, their questions made some sense. How could he presume to lead them if he insisted on violating their norms?

But the question they should have been asking was, "Who is he?" If he is Messiah and his disciples stray from certain norms, what does that say about the norms? Is he, in fact, fulfilling the Law and the Prophets by urging his people away from fussy traditions and toward servanthood ministries like healing the sick? Should we be learning from him, rather than judging him?

> How could he presume to lead them if he insisted on violating their norms?

But that isn't humanity's normal way. Congregations greet new pastors, not by hearing the new word they bring, but by demanding that they adapt to local customs. Children in newly blended families want things to stay the same. We don't exhibit much curiosity about other people and how they can be known through their choices, accents, interests, and experiences. We tend to ask questions that start with "Why don't?"

Christians sometimes muster the courage to be different. But in my experience, most assemblies want to fit in. They want to be liked and respected. They resist challenging anyone, because the challenged can strike back or take their money elsewhere.

Instead, Christians have been energetic setters and enforcers of societal norms. Rather than encourage uniqueness and diversity, we have insisted on conformity, generally conformity to whatever the ruling interests want. The liturgically minded fight over which words will be said around the world, as if local needs, accents, and personalities didn't exist. Fundamentalists demand uniform interpretations, as if all persons should live in the same intellectual and theological "room."

The people could have learned so much from Jesus if they had asked him to explain, not to defend. But attack comes more naturally than curiosity.

Listening

John 6:37: [Jesus said], "Everything that the Father gives me will come to me, and anyone who comes to me I will never drive away."

My twenty-two-year-old son returns safely from nine days in Europe. He regales us with tales of flights and trains, hostels, baguettes and brie in Paris, cheering the Tour de France outside the Louvre, climbing a hill to scan Nice at night, discovering Rome on foot, falling in love with London, chatting with folks at a pub, and wanting to go back for a longer stay.

Our entire family gathers to listen. We have news, too, but this is his moment, his return in triumph. We pepper him with questions. His answers build bridges to our own memories. But we try to avoid the common conversational gambit of pouncing on the speaker's detail to turn the spotlight back to self. Every adventurer deserves a time of telling.

It would be unthinkable for us to refuse to listen. Or to disparage his adventure as inferior to our own. Or to moan enviously. Or to find fault in his rejoicing.

Our part is to know our delight at his return and to give him room to celebrate. Our turn will come. We don't need to be anxious about losing the spotlight.

The same dynamics would hold true if he had come home in defeat. Perhaps more so. He would need time for telling and room for mourning.

I say "unthinkable," but in fact we mishandle such moments all too frequently. We seize the spotlight, we refuse to listen, and we criticize. We listen selectively, allowing room for those who can benefit our self-interest—listening to a boss, for example—and turn a less patient ear to children, underlings, and the familiar.

We sometimes have no room at all for the annoying, the powerless, the stranger, and the needy.

But, then, we are human, trapped in frailties and self-destructive tendencies, only sporadically able to get outside ourselves, likely to see all reality through eyes clouded by fear and self-loathing.

What about God? Does God share our unwillingness to listen, our instinct for rejection, our manic hunger for the spotlight? Does God dominate every conversation for fear of losing control and feeling small? Does God turn a deaf ear to tales of triumph or defeat? Does God never miss an opening to find fault?

Now that would be unthinkable. Who would want a God who had no room for the other, no patience for listening, whose self-esteem was so meager as to require endless reassurances, whose ego was so overblown as to demand control? Who would want a God who sent away all but a few?

If Jesus made nothing else clear, it was that God isn't like us. In love with us, yes, but with a love that is larger than anything we can muster. Nothing conveys that otherness of God more clearly than Jesus' attitude toward strangers and outcasts, his unwavering determination to embrace all of humanity, and to do so without the conditions that we impose, including those conditions that we call "God's will."

> *We say we are defending God, when in fact we are defending ourselves.*

Believers spend lifetimes debating who is allowed to come close, who is worthy to receive, who must be made to change. We are masters at devising litmus tests, barriers, questions that must be answered correctly, merit badges that must be earned. Whether we close the door with overt "standards" or the raised eyebrow of scorn, we don't hesitate to send people away unheard, unseen, unloved.

We say we are defending God, when in fact we are defending ourselves. We say we are "loving the sinner," as if one could feel loved by being rejected and made to feel dirty. We say we are honoring Scripture, as if our grasp of God's word were the only grasp.

In fact, driving people away makes us feel safe and large. But Jesus had a different word: "Anyone who comes to me I will never drive away."

Judgment

Mark 2:6-7: Now some of the scribes were sitting there, questioning in their hearts, "Why does this fellow speak in this way? It is blasphemy! Who can forgive sins but God alone?"

As a hundred or so men, women, and children file past our serving line at the Homeless Shelter, it would be easy to judge them.

"Why don't they get jobs?" Well, most do have jobs. They cook at fast-food restaurants, collect trash, do day labor. Maybe we should judge those who set minimum wage policy.

"Why can't they find housing?" Well, many do have homes. They just don't have enough left over to buy food. The rest had homes at one time. But life got rough, partly through their own poor choices, partly through circumstance.

"Why can't they stop drinking and doing drugs?" Good question. Addiction is a powerful force. But it seems to me we should save some judgment for those who prey on the populace and would be happy to hook all of us on booze and drugs.

"Why do these women keep having babies if they can't afford to care for them?" Ask the men who impregnate them. Ask the morality police who refuse to make birth-control devices and education available to them. Yes, the women bear responsibility, too. They endure the consequences every hour of the day.

"Why are so many homeless people African American?" We could spend our lives puzzling through that question. Many black people do. The answers would break our hearts. A bigoted society destroys lives at every level.

Judgment, in other words, is easier to voice than to justify. In fact, judgment comes naturally, immediately, whenever we see someone behaving outside our expectations or comfort. Judgment is a self-defense.

We can get high and mighty and label our judgments as "God's judgment." We can prowl the Scriptures to document our judgments. We can elevate our judgments to doctrines and rules. But, the fact remains, we are simply protecting ourselves. We see diversity, change, someone else's frailty, our own frailty, an unexpected event or person, and we pass judgment as a way of building a wall against it.

Discernment is another matter. Discernment sees the same realities and might be just as troubled by them, but discernment seeks to understand, not to distance. Discernment asks why, but not to label or to disparage. Discernment wants to grow in wisdom and to make loving response. Discernment is concerned for the other.

Discernment comes across as weak, of course, because discernment rarely settles on simple explanations or solutions. Judgment is much more fun.

> *Judgment is a self-defense.*

In the incident recorded by Mark, the scribes saw something outside their tidy world. They asked why, but immediately answered their own question, "It is blasphemy." They judged, rather than exercise discernment. If they had allowed Jesus to answer the "why," they might have learned something.

Throughout his ministry, Jesus presented this same problem to all who met him. He was different, he was beyond their boundaries, he said words that startled, and did deeds that amazed and frightened. We have tried to tame Jesus in the predictable and controllable confines of religion. But even now he still breaks free, as he certainly did in every encounter of his ministry.

The question then becomes: do we judge, or do we discern? We will inevitably ask, "Why?" But will we then listen to God's answer or construct our own?

Our own answers generally feel better. God's answers tend to push us on to other questions, eventually forcing us to confront ourselves, our values, our behavior, our capacity for love and hate, our lusts and pride.

Judgment tries to forestall that difficult and painful work of self-examination. Discernment takes the risk of lingering in the why.

Self

John 12:25: [Jesus said], "Those who love their life lose it, and those who hate their life in this world will keep it for eternal life."

As our conference ends and attendees start to scatter, a colleague, prospective client, and I stay an extra afternoon to play golf on one of Disney World's five courses. It feels liberating to be away from our convention hotel, away from noise and name badges, away from deals and software. Not that any golf course is a walk through virgin fields. But at least it is quiet.

Even so, it takes me ten holes to relax. This conference has left me on edge. Some of that edginess would happen at any week-long business conference. But some has to do with this setting and its unrelenting theme of "I."

A local advertisement puts it this way: "Everything here is about you." Or, if one is on the receiving end, "Everything here is about me."

From sunup to sundown, from lobby to latte, from meeting room to manicured lawn, the message is "self." Disney has trained its staff well. They give good smile. But there is a reason that staff quarters refer to employees as the "cast." They are acting. Their reality has been checked at some outlying door. One doesn't connect with them. Even the simplest question evokes a rehearsed answer. "They are always on message," says a friend.

Some find Disney World's focus on self-pleasuring delightful. The price of flattery might be steep, but it is probably a welcome respite from hierarchical workplaces where perks and privileges are reserved for others.

But the cumulative effect is wearing. I watch people lose touch with the first person plural. Conference-goers who arrived in teams start to speak only of "I." Instead of drawing closer, people seem to fragment. Meetings seem surprisingly lifeless, because listening or discussing requires loss of focus on "I."

People become prickly. I feel myself becoming prickly. The normal valences by which we connect seem to shrivel up here, as if each person has gone solo and is thinking, If this conversation isn't about me, then something is wrong.

It is marvelous, therefore, when our golf foursome starts to loosen and to connect. We laugh and listen. We get outside ourselves. When we return for one last Disney dinner, the waiter's rehearsed flattery comes across as absurd.

Self is a powerful engine. It can be all-consuming, as we see in children. To get beyond self requires energy, discipline, and maturity. Our culture gives us little encouragement, for self-pleasure-seekers are earnest consumers and malleable employees, easily flattered and controlled.

> *I watch people lose touch with the first person plural. Conference-goers who arrived in teams start to speak only of "I."*

The irony— tragic irony—is that life works exactly as Jesus said. Those who serve only themselves eventually lose their freedom, lose their integrity, lose their enjoyment of life, and lose their souls.

A year ago, when they announced that Disney World would be the site of this year's annual conference, people cheered with delight. As the reality of pervasive nonreality set in, I saw delight dwindle and vanish. Not for everyone, of course. But I saw more and more people walking around alone, watching the clock, moving restlessly from event to event. Few came to an awards ceremony. A banquet fell flat because people rushed the food line 30 minutes early, so they could eat and be gone.

Jesus said, "Those who love their life will lose it." And that is precisely what happens. Self-serving leads to despair, for no amount of flattery or funnel cake can fill the chasm opened by self-pleasuring.

We'll probably recover from seven days in manicured artifice. But Disney knows its audience. Disney is us. Catering to self isn't a Disney malady. It is the darkness we all inhabit. To escape the darkness, we must resist the tempter's siren song of "I."

Balance

John 6:11: Then Jesus took the loaves, and when he had given thanks, he distributed them to those who were seated; so also the fish, as much as they wanted.

The term "cognitive dissonance" comes to mind. Or maybe just the word "strange." But after spending five days with my parents—mother in the hospital, father preparing to live alone—I now find myself in the pastel, unfailingly cheerful, and squeaky-clean world of Walt Disney Company. No beeping monitors here, no pureed food, no walks down the hall carrying an oxygen tank, no trying to make a cell phone call in the solarium as a psychotic woman talks violently to herself.

Here parents tote children exhausted by the day's fun at Disney World. Here Goofy and Pluto lumber around the dining room dispensing four-fingered hugs. Here everything works, everyone smiles, and a piano player sits in a vast and empty rotunda playing tunes that would be more recognizable if I had devoted my childhood to Disney films.

My colleagues and I are here for a week-long conference. Our best strategy, we decide, is to go with the flow, let it happen, relax, and let Mickey be Mickey. (Maybe the next conference will be in, say, Calgary, where we can see something real, like wheat or a rodeo.)

The clinical answer to "cognitive dissonance"—a conflict between incompatible beliefs or actions—is to abandon one of the beliefs or behaviors. I don't find that reality is quite so tidy. One often just stands in the middle, balancing, without much leverage for resolving anything.

So it is that I laugh with my colleagues as Goofy startles a woman in midsentence, and then my cell phone rings and my father reports the day's medical news, and then I return to a discussion of the impoverished Christian aesthetic. I wonder how many disparate worlds a person can inhabit at one time.

I do know this: one needs to try for balance. Reality is a messy affair. Disney tries to make everything orderly and predictable. So do we at home, at work, at church. I suspect we would love to focus on just one thing and leave the rest for later. But like nurses and therapists at a busy hospital, reality keeps on intruding, forcing itself on us—today, for example, reminding me that a parent is gravely ill, a child is playing soccer, a house is being built, a war is under way, a promising contract requires my attention, a client needs answers, Duke is losing to Kansas, and I am surrounded by lamps shaped like flowers.

I can't make any of these conflicting realities go away. So what do I do? What Jesus did was to feed his people. All of them, each in his or her unique hunger. He didn't require anything of them, such as uniformity of belief, consistency of doctrine, perfection of ritual, or any of the myriad credentials and hoops that Christians have required of each other. He simply saw the hungers, took what was at hand, asked God's blessing on it, and gave food.

> *Balance is submission, letting go of control, and allowing oneself to be fed.*

He didn't soothe them by resolving his message of repentance—talk about "cognitive dissonance"—with a cheerful smile. His word after the food was as difficult to hear as his word before. Reality didn't evaporate. What Jesus did was to feed the weary traveler.

Balance, then, isn't an act of cleverness or skillful multitasking. Balance is submission, letting go of control, and allowing oneself to be fed. Maybe cheerful desk clerks are part of that, but more likely we need work friends who ask about our home lives, and partners who ask about our work, and parents who send us forward to live even as they are dying, and at least a glimmer of perspective, for flower-shaped lamps are simply decor.

Jumble

John 6:48-50: [Jesus said], "I am the bread of life. Your ancestors ate the manna in the wilderness, and they died. This is the bread that comes down from heaven, so that one may eat of it and not die."

After a week at home editing a book manuscript and poking around the used-car market, I find that my study is a jumble.

I count seven stacks of papers, plus scattered notes and mail, plus a mind swirling with slippery details and questions. It's time for sorting and closure. Sort the edits, sort the printouts of car data, make notes, make decisions.

It is time, in other words, for focus. See what needs to be seen, decide what needs to be decided, and set the rest aside.

But is that real? Or even possible? And if it were possible to turn off all distractions—stop the newspaper, turn off e-mail and telephone, ignore competing claims, ignore other voices, avoid conversations on other topics—would that be right? How would God get through? How can one be a servant if the door is closed?

The focused mind is a powerful force. If you concentrate your energies on a single task, you can do wonders. If you harness political energies to a single cause, you can prevail over the scattered. Single-minded ambition, single-threaded performance, single-issue politics—they all work.

But reality is so much more complex and distracting. Your favorite cause is only one cause among many, and perhaps not as important as others. For you to win, someone else must lose, and living alongside vote-count losers is inevitably complicating.

Joy, truth, and meaning tend to be surprises. The art of living isn't to freeze the kaleidoscope, but to remain nimble and curious. The tightly focused mind tends to yield weakness, not strength.

That's why single-issue politicians are so effective in running for office and so inept and dangerous when governing. That's why couples often do better at falling in love than in living together. It's why people do better at arguing than listening.

As convention-goers discover after focusing energy on what they deem critical decisions, it is easier to make decisions than to live into them. Counting votes is easier than counting the cost. Declaring the outcome of a highly focused debate is easier than rediscovering complexities that were temporarily shoved aside.

When the Hebrews were crossing the wilderness, their leader Moses had a single-track focus: keep them moving toward Canaan, do whatever it took to keep them from turning back to bondage. For a time, God seemed to share that focus. Hence cloud and fire to give them direction, tablets of Law to guide their common life, and manna to give them sustenance.

> *The art of living isn't to freeze the kaleidoscope, but to remain nimble and curious.*

Once they emerged from the wilderness, however, they needed to find their own way, make their own decisions, and plant their own grain. Not because God had abandoned them, but because faith ultimately is choices, and the only durable faith—the only faith capable of being a "beacon to the nations"—is the faith which learns to see all of reality and to shine in all directions.

Christians are tempted to see Jesus as the new Moses, single-mindedly leading his people to a single destination; and to see the church as the new Israel-in-Sinai, a beleaguered tribe facing harsh elements and needing to remain focused.

Jesus himself, however, was anything but a single-track mind. He wandered from place to place. He moved restlessly from one idea to another. To his disciples' dismay, he opened his embrace to all manner of people. He affirmed the Law but then departed from it. He upheld tradition but then violated it. His friends and enemies tried to pin him down to a defining word. He dodged and resisted.

Jesus wasn't the new Moses. He refused to promulgate laws or to rule by decree. His followers weren't the new Israel-in-Sinai, forming a single column and marching eastward across the desert. They were to scatter, to be a servant people, to hear many voices, to touch many lives, and always to die to self.

The church's eventual decision to form hierarchies capped by imperial rulers and to focus on selected thoughts, selected people, and selected actions was a perversion of what Jesus seemed to intend. It has had tragic consequences, not the least of which is our current fascination with single-track issues to the exclusion of all else.

Forgiveness

John 20:22-23: [Jesus] breathed on [the disciples] and said to them, "Receive the Holy Spirit. If you forgive the sins of any, they are forgiven them; if you retain the sins of any, they are retained."

I do a final review on TurboTax, save files, print forms, write checks, affix ample postage, and put two bulky envelopes in the mailbox. Done for another year.

When you think about it, the U.S. tax system is remarkable. Instead of confiscation, we calculate our own taxes. Instead of continual levies to pay for royal adventures, we do taxes once a year. Despite constant pressure from the wealthy to get unfair advantage, the tax burden is intended to be equitable.

Some individuals cheat, but most seem to do the honest thing. Corporations show less savory performance, with their off-shore schemes and costly lobbying. But citizens eventually remember that if a few plunder, the whole system will collapse.

Behind the scenes, of course, is the weight of law. The fact that I compile my own records and work from the comfort of my home computer doesn't mean that I am in total control. I don't set the rules. My control takes place within a context. If I abuse my freedom, I can expect consequences.

A similar situation applies to the authority Jesus gave to his disciples.

Our Lord's intent wasn't entirely clear. Jesus seems to have given little thought to any institution being founded in his name. Mainly he was concerned that the men and women surrounding him be committed to continuing his ministry. They were the "sent." He didn't transmit rules or structures, but rather gave them words (parables mostly) to remember and examples of accepting new life as servants.

Such a vague and self-denying commission didn't sit well with would-be leaders. So they made much of Matthew's account of Jesus' giving the "keys" to Peter and of John's account of disciples' receiving authority to dispense forgiveness. Even though the Gospels, as a whole, don't support such aims, they built an institution grounded in absolute authority (the supreme leader eventually being considered the very mouth of God) and in laws defining salvation and belonging.

We are free, of course, to create whatever institution we want, even one that bears little resemblance to how Jesus lived. We are free to splinter into countless denominations or to coalesce into a worldwide institution. We are free to create movies, novels, doctrines, even daily meditations that purport to convey truth. We are free to do whatever we want on Sunday morning, to ignore religious obligation entirely, or to place our bets on last-minute repentance.

> *Our freedom, like our compliance with the tax code, takes place within a context.*

But our freedom, like our compliance with the tax code, takes place within a context. Behind the institutions we create lies God's actual intent. Our rules and protocols don't define ultimate reality. Our standards for dispensing holy benefits don't determine God's grace. We can call our structures "holy" and "apostolic," but God's trajectory through history takes its own course.

Take, for example, the forgiveness authority cited by John. At first glance, Jesus appears to give his disciples authority to separate sheep from goats, to reward some and punish others, maybe even to set the rules of forgiveness.

But is that what Jesus meant? The larger message of forgiveness, you see, is that God is infinitely patient and merciful, that God welcomes all to the banquet (even though we are free not to come), that God's desire is to embrace, not to exclude.

Exclusion is our way, not God's. Excommunication, labeling, inquisitions, banning, shunning, membership votes, and our standard-setting for who's in and who's out—those are our ways, not God's way.

If the disciples were given any authority, it was a charge to do it God's way. That is, to forgive extravagantly, to love without condition, to form circles of inclusion. We might prefer to be parsimonious with mercy, but that, like cheating on taxes, leads to consequences not of our choosing.

Silence

Luke 24:4-5: While they were perplexed about this, suddenly two men in dazzling clothes stood beside them. The women were terrified and bowed their faces to the ground.

Tonight's soccer game is great, but I tarnish it by talking too much. I honor my vow to refrain from yelling at players, especially my son. But I keep a sotto voce commentary going with my wife, most of it praising our kids for learning to pass and to play positions, but some of it lamenting their play.

Two comments concern forwards. One is considerably overweight and cannot keep up with the attack. I mention his need to lose weight. The other concerns a forward who is quick but won't press the attack. Our team misses several scoring opportunities because these two are lagging.

After the 2-1 loss, both players come to their parents, who happen to be sitting nearby and surely overheard my comments. I immediately regret my commentary.

Lesson: figure out which kids go with which parents. Larger lesson: be quiet.

At some point in the faith journey, this becomes the operative word: be quiet. Our worldly noise drowns out the still, small voice of God. Our personal wordiness makes no room for hearing. Even prayer can get in the way. Sometimes it is necessary just to bow our faces to the ground and let God say what needs to be said.

That is off-center behavior for believers, because our faith is primarily a matter of words. We read words, write words, gather to hear and to sing words, admire graceful words, reward effective wordsmiths in the pulpit, and, when need arises, respond with words. Our words range from the careful and intellectual to the wild and emotional. But words tend to be our bridge to each other and to God.

At some point, however, our words stand between us and God. We phrase prayers with language that soothes our spirits, but is that God's intent? We proclaim truths that make sense of what we know, but is that God's sense? We study words of Scripture, but are they God's living word?

We will never know unless we stop talking and allow a silence for God to fill. The women at the tomb were driven to that silence, first, by discovery of a missing body, and second, by the appearance of angels. They were terrified and perplexed. In response, they bowed their faces to the ground.

Then the angels could speak. Then they could explain the missing body. Then they could remind the women what Jesus had said during his ministry. Then the women had something to say.

Note that the apostles dismissed the women's words as an "idle tale" until they went to the tomb and themselves were driven to silence.

> *Our words are ultimately about control.*

A reader asks why God won't speak to her. There is a lifetime context for her question and no simple answers. But I would commend her to silence. I don't mean that silence which listens impatiently for an expected word, or that silence which seizes an opening to resume talking, but silence like that on Easter morning. Silence as emptiness, silence as being in the presence of something that one's own words cannot comprehend, silence as letting go of control.

Our words are ultimately about control. That's why we talk so much. Words enable us to control other people—hence the tendency of weak bosses to dominate meetings with their words, rather than listening for fresh information. Words enable us to control reality—hence our tendency to categorize, compartmentalize, judge, define. Words enable us to hide and to avoid.

Faith is about letting go of such control.

Self-Emptying

Luke 24:6-8: The men said, "Remember how he told you, while he was still in Galilee, that the Son of Man must be handed over to sinners, and be crucified, and on the third day rise again." Then they remembered his words.

Humility piles on humility as I work with my older sons to launch a Web site that will support and supplement these daily e-mailed meditations.

I am writing the content, but they—ages 24 and 23—are doing the heavy lifting: programming the site's functionality, setting up security, arranging certificates, preparing "Terms and Conditions," and turning my efforts into pages viewable on any browser.

My job is to listen to them. They work in the field of Web programming. They know how to stitch together a Web site. I know where I want to end up, but it is their knowledge that will get us there.

This is a reversal, of course. It wasn't long ago that I had the knowledge and they were listening. But they are older and more experienced now. Life and hard work have given them skills different from mine. I must abandon any illusion of parental omnipotence and listen to what they say.

A reader asks for practical guidance on dying in order to live. What did Jesus mean by that? A good question for Good Friday. A better question, in my view, than how much blood Jesus shed or how deeply the scourging cut.

On Easter morning, angels told the women two things: First, they explained the empty tomb: "He is not here, but has risen." Second, they urged the women to "remember" what Jesus had told them. Jesus had seen this coming and knew it was necessary.

This, in my view, is where the divinity of Jesus is manifest: not in supernatural powers, but in having been there before, in having been betrayed in the Garden of Eden, whined against in distress, forgotten in the thrill of victory, turned into weapon, partisan, curse and book, consulted when convenient, loved intermittently, and now rejected in the flesh.

Jesus knew, and he told his friends. It was now on them to listen. That, dear reader, is where dying to self starts. Not in being nice, loving, generous, or friendly, but in knowing one's need to listen outside ourselves. We don't know it all, cannot imagine it all, cannot study enough, or invent enough, or calculate enough. We know a lot, but God knows more, and the people around us know more, too.

Some of our listening hearkens backward to events recorded in Scripture and emulated in Tradition. But we must listen also to life. And that is a humbling task. We must bend the knee of pride and listen to spouses, children, neighbors, and enemies. We must listen to voices that make us uncomfortable. We must allow God to call our treasured institutions and folkways into question. We must listen for the new accents, restless yearnings, and evolving presence of a living God.

> *When you choose to listen, you lose control.*

When you choose to listen, you lose control. God may be quite different from the convenient pictures we have painted. Our doctrines might be 100 percent about us, merely clever ways not to listen. Our traditions might answer questions that God never intended to ask.

Dying to self isn't like taking a course, where you know syllabus and requirements in advance. Dying to self is like falling in love, leaving home, or bearing children: you don't know where you are going, how you will get there, whom you will meet along the way, or what you will find.

Faith is a venture in self-emptying, not self-fulfillment.

PART FOUR

Hope

I want to believe and to trust;

I want to love and to be loved.

So does God.

Therefore, we both have hope.

Christmas

John 1:3b-5: What has come into being in him was life, and the light was the light of all people. The light shines in the darkness, and the darkness did not overcome it.

My home world is quiet and peaceful. A Christmas tree surrounded by gifts awaits the waking of my family. Brightly wrapped gifts display tokens of our love for each other.

On the radio, I listen to Bach's *Christmas Oratorio*, Pavarotti singing "Adeste Fideles," a German choir singing "Silent Night," and now a soprano and strings singing "Ave Maria."

Outside, a rainstorm is hanging on in the darkness. It will be no day for the family Christmas walk.

Outside, more than rain is dampening human spirits. The news lately has been almost uniformly grim—looming war in Iraq, nuclear saber-rattling by North Korea, China's steady squelching of Hong Kong, tribal slaughter in Nigeria, bankruptcy and political chaos throughout South America, gloom in Bethlehem, the unrelenting acid of Islamic terrorism and our own racism, continued coarsening of our culture, a limping economy, spreading layoffs, and widespread retreats into mood-altering and appearance-altering.

Outside, some households will awaken to a harsh light. Children won't be showered with love, abundance, or even enough food. Children will awaken to troubled adults, some of whom try bravely to protect their children from grownup troubles, some of whom don't hesitate to visit their anger on the young.

Outside, many adults will wake up alone—woefully alone, exactly the opposite of what they hoped for in life.

Outside, many adults will share gifts that they couldn't afford to buy. Many will weep inside at the job losses that require lean giving. Many will yearn for the gentler days when they were children and someone else bore such burdens.

Outside, there is darkness. And to be honest, there is darkness inside at times, too, not as much darkness as others must endure, but still the doubts and wants and fears that ever shadow the human condition.

Long ago, God's Word became flesh and dwelled among us. In him was life, and his life was light to all of this darkness. The darkness of his own brutal day, the darkness of every age since then, and now the darkness of our own.

We yearn for that light. Every day, at some level of our being, we awaken and hope today will be better. We hope for food, for work, for companionship, for an end to brutality and hatred, for common sense and tolerance.

> *I believe that humanity's yearning—all of it, the wailing and the wishing, the eagerness and the edginess—is somehow, in the mind of a loving God, bound together into a single reaching for the light.*

We yearn for Messiah. We might not give our yearning that name. But I believe that humanity's yearning—all of it, the wailing and the wishing, the eagerness and the edginess—is somehow, in the mind of a loving God, bound together into a single reaching for the light.

"For unto us a child is born," sing the sopranos next to me. The tenors join, and the altos, and now the basses, my part in Handel's jubilation, all leading into a unison rejoicing shout: "Wonderful Counselor! The Mighty God! The Everlasting Father! The Prince of Peace!"

"And the government shall be upon his shoulders." Not on our shoulders, not on our warring princes of politics and religion, not on the predators who steal our hopes, not on the frailty by which we wound even those whom we love, not on our memories or stirrings, not on our gift-laden trees or tear-stained hearts.

Life and light aren't up to us. They never were, and they aren't now. God has held us in the palm of his hand from long before we craved holding. God whispered love to us before we knew any aching. God turned away from wrath before we had begged forgiveness. God sent his Son while we were sleeping.

And now, as we dare to awaken, God's light shines bravely, and the darkness will never overcome it!

Believe

John 1:49-51: Nathanael replied, "Rabbi, you are the Son of God! You are the King of Israel!" Jesus answered, "Do you believe because I told you that I saw you under the fig tree? You will see greater things than these." And he said to him, "Very truly, I tell you, you will see heaven opened and the angels of God ascending and descending upon the Son of Man."

In the course of a day, I see things that ancients could never have imagined. I talk across the ocean with a man in London. I exchange written messages almost at the speed of light. I write, edit, and send without leaving my seat. I check my bank account without bothering a teller.

I drive a four-wheeled vehicle at 70 miles per hour, enter a huge metal tube and am carried at 30,000 feet to a city 700 miles away in two hours, buy a "Greek salad" in Detroit that bears no resemblance to anything Hellenic, board another metal tube, fly through more air, call my family by holding a small device to my ear, and meet my sister and brother-in-law in a corridor.

Having witnessed these sights come of age during my lifetime, I know they are testimony to human creativity and diligence, but I doubt they point especially to God. For God's power doesn't reside in moving metal or electrons.

Maybe God's power can be found here: I enter the door of my parents' home and there, standing upright, is my mother. Still tethered to an oxygen machine, but a far cry from the semi-comatose hospital patient I last saw fighting for her life after acquiring West Nile virus.

Now here is a miracle worthy of prayer. Her medical care was like airplanes and e-mail: testimony to human capability, developed over time, and amazing in every respect. But her grit, her determination to live, her gratitude at being back in her home, my father's steadfast vigil at her bedside for three-and-a-half months, and my own astonishment and gratitude—now, those are of God.

Those can cause one to believe, that is, to suspend normal judgments, to look beyond the last visible star, to imagine a force not measured in speed or heft, to think of life as meaning more than what our hands can grasp, to trust in a fundamental goodness.

Nathanael saw a parlor trick. That's all. And yet on the basis of that, he proclaimed Jesus "Son of God." How could his response not be shallow, grounded as it was in a minor gesture? Could this fawning disciple truly give his life away on such meager evidence?

No, said Jesus, he would see "greater things than these." He would see more miracles, for the Gospel of John is structured as an account of "signs." But more than that—far more than that—he would see the love and compassion of God, the mercy and forgiveness that humanity can never quite muster. He would see a man born blind regain his sight, but even more than gaining sight, the man and his parents would gain courage to stand up to the darkness.

> It is when you see the weak stand tall, the losers win, the oppressed go free, the lost be found, the proud grow humble, and one's own knee bend in gratitude

He would see Jesus rise from the dead, but even more, he would see Jesus die. He would see Calvary. He would see an innocent man bear the suffering of humanity onto the hard wood of the cross.

If he looked closely, Nathanael would see his own life change, his own heart grow strong for justice and mercy, his own path become new. He would see himself aligned against evil and those who profit from evil. He would see his friendships change. He would become a new creation.

"Greater things," you see, aren't about speed, height, distance, money, parlor tricks, or thrones. It is when you see the weak stand tall, the losers win, the oppressed go free, the lost be found, the proud grow humble, and one's own kness bend in gratitude— that is when you have cause to believe.

Convention

John 6:27: [Jesus answered the crowd] "Do not work for the food that perishes, but for the food that endures for eternal life, which the Son of Man will give you."

It is too much, I suppose, to expect an outbreak of common sense at the Episcopal Church General Convention opening today* in Minneapolis.

Or an outbreak of tolerance. Or mutual respect. Or good biblical scholarship. Or enlightened debate. Or anything approaching the gospel.

Instead, the angry and self-righteous will parade to microphones in full harrumph. They will heap abuse on Scripture by reading it through a fine sieve of doctrinal and cultural prejudice. They will heap abuse on their opponents, as if Satan stood at the opposing microphone. They will threaten to leave—as if they had someplace to go, as if there were a lively market in disenchanted Episcopalians.

Delegates and visitors will ignore what Jesus did say—a nice hotel and dinner reservations not being a promising context for Jesus' teachings on wealth and self-sacrifice. Instead, they will summon fresh vitriol for topics that were of no discernible interest to Jesus but dominate the Church's life.

Meanwhile, out there are people like you and me, who awoke this morning worried not about the sexual orientation of a bishop-elect, but about the schools our children attend, our troubled communities, a marketplace ruled by short-sighted greed, a government ruled by secrecy and self-serving, a culture promoting obesity and escape.

We woke up to ourselves and all that delights and ails us. We woke up to first love and lost love. We woke up feeling perky or panicked. Fewer have jobs than had them three years ago, when

*The author is referring to the General Convention held July 30–August 8, 2003.

85

General Convention last gathered. Fewer have financial stability. Fewer feel secure in their homeland. Fewer know where their children of military age were last night.

We woke up to reality, and that is where Jesus meets us, bearing "food that endures for eternal life." As our days proceed, we might join convention-goers in unreality—in faux scholarship pretending to be the real thing, in impassioned but sterile debates, in parades that celebrate style, in seeing the other as a danger. But at the end of the day, reality will reintroduce itself, and once again we will find our Savior waiting to feed us.

> *At the end of the day, reality will reintroduce itself, and once again we will find our Savior waiting to feed us.*

Despite all that was said in his name, Jesus will hold out his hand to every one of us—not just the doctrinally pure or properly elected—and he will ask about our days, not about our debates, and he will offer a helping hand, not a clenched fist.

While the proud and unflinching claim to speak for our interests, we will gather what we know to be true and offer it up to God. Our prayers might lack style or solid theology. We will ache for something as simple as a smile. We will weep over life, not over religion.

But God will catch our tears, savor our smiles, and "keep watch with those who work, or watch, or weep this night, and give angels charge over those who sleep." Our Savior will "stay with us" and be "our companion in the way."*

And not an angry word spoken in Minneapolis can change that. No harrumphing will turn God's heart to vengeance. No quoting of Leviticus will make God intolerant. And no quest for power and right opinion will thwart God's determination to lead us beside still waters.

Maybe I will be proved wrong about Convention. Maybe the warriors of Minneapolis will turn their tortured scriptures to plowshares and their vote-tally sheets to pruning hooks. Maybe they will stand at microphones and simply confess their sins. Maybe they will drop their stones and pick up song sheets. And from lips pursed tightly will come a simple plea: "Help of the helpless, O abide with me.'"

*The Book of Common Prayer, pp. 114 and 139.
†"Abide With Me," The Hymnal 1982, p. 662.

New Situation

Mark 5:22-23: One of the leaders of the synagogue named Jairus came and, when he saw [Jesus], fell at his feet and begged him repeatedly, "My little daughter is at the point of death. Come and lay your hands on her, so that she may be made well, and live."

I open my study windows to let in morning air and notice three crows feasting on the grass seed that I scattered yesterday. They hear me and fly away. I listen to them cawing from the trees.

If this were grain and my family's livelihood, I might be upset. But it is just a lawn and, given the onset of summer heat, not a venture with much chance of succeeding. Our house was finished too late for spring planting.

Yesterday morning, as I was sitting down to breakfast, my youngest son was picked up for a week at Boy Scout camp. He was nervous. Which mattered more: eating breakfast while it was fresh or sending my son off with a hug?

Same thing at dinner. One of our middle son's best friends joined us for dinner. Should we stick to our evening routines or welcome him to our table? While we were eating, my father called to check in. Should I stay at the table or take the call?

Those aren't difficult choices. For we recognize that some things matter more than others. But how far are we willing to take that recognition?

When "situational ethics" appeared on the scene several years ago, it bothered many who wanted hard-and-fast moral codes applicable to every situation. "Situational ethics" became a favorite target for fundamentalists.

Well, how about "situational faith"? Now there's a topic to stress the rigid. Could it be that the pillars of faith need to bend in the wind? Could it be that the "fundamentals" of faith aren't doctrines, formulas, and rules, or even consistent interpretations of Scripture, but accessibility to unfolding reality and a willingness to change course?

Look first at Jairus. Here was a leader of the religious establishment, the very people who felt most threatened by Jesus' ministry. They taught in complex certainties; Jesus taught in ambiguous parables. They had clear rules for every situation; Jesus took each situation as it came. They defended a house built on ancient tradition; Jesus moved about like a nomad. They clung to ritual; Jesus invented new ways. They told people what to believe; Jesus wept over the people's suffering.

> *What changed? His daughter's illness created a new situation.*

Now came Jairus begging for Jesus' help. What changed? His daughter's illness created a new situation. A father's love was stronger than religion. If Jesus had the power to heal his daughter, then consistency must be set aside.

In the same way, Jesus changed his plans. He was moving about— teaching when he could, dodging premature danger. But when he heard Jairus's plea, he set aside his plans and went with Jairus.

In retrospect, we say, "Of course. What else could Jesus do?" Precisely. Situations change, and situations require fresh faith. Why, then, do we cling to pillars of faith that we, not Jesus, erected? From start to finish, Jesus promulgated no doctrines, and yet we insist on defining Christianity to the finest degree. Jesus adopted no rituals, and yet we obsess about the sanctity of our rituals. Jesus moved about like a nomad, while we talk of "planting" churches.

We judge each other by formulas and are deaf to faith's ever-changing accents. We stay indoors, while the world outside is suffering.

But the day will come when, like Jairus, we find too little healing in the established pillars of faith and we cry out instead for a living God. Some things will matter more than others. What will we then expect: a God who says, "I'm busy," or a God who sets aside everything in order to love?

Rain

John 15:17: [Jesus said], "I am giving you these commandments so that you may love one another."

A nd then there are the "dumb days." Those are the days when the stars and stressors line up, like tumblers in a lock, allowing free entry to woes and wants.

Those are the days when rain falls again and water's gift of life is lost amid worries about planting and schedules. Or, if one is resident in Arizona, not enough rain falls, and wildfires threaten.

Those are the days when e-mail brings assault, a knot tightens in one's chest, and peace seems elusive. Even the smallest decision seems questionable, and whether to leave a dinner party produces a rush of second-guessing.

Such is my day today.

I stand on a building site where the inside is ready for occupancy but the outside is soupy mud. I sense more delays coming, pushing us three months behind schedule. The tumblers align, nine months of aggravation charge like a rhino, and I wonder aloud, "Is this house cursed?" My mind knows it isn't, but my heart gives voice to accumulated frustration.

Where is this assault coming from? I ask after enduring a string of attack e-mails from someone who thinks me incompetent and unworthy. I can't just shrug it off. Maybe I am not "tough" enough. Maybe at some level I share his doubts. I just know the knot in my chest won't go away.

I read enough newspapers and friends' e-mail to know that my "dumb day" barely registers on a cosmic scale of woe. But knowing that others have it worse is rarely solace. I still must deal with today.

And so I turn, as countless times before, to my wife. I vent, she listens. What a gift. No solutions, no chorus of blame-the-other, no competition for sympathy airtime. As Paul wrote to arrogant Corinthians, "Love is patient; love is kind."

I rely on the patience of friends. The dinner party is going well, but I cannot sit still any longer, I cannot keep making conversation. I want to remain, but my jumbled innards say, Go. I need them to accept.

Rain returns this morning. But then comes a hymn on the radio. "What a friend we have in Jesus," sings a fine choir. "Jesus knows our every weakness; take it to the Lord in prayer!"

An immigrant to Canada named Joseph Scriven wrote that text in 1855 to comfort his mother back in Ireland. Also to comfort himself, for he had lost one fiancée to drowning on the night before their wedding and a second fiancée to illness shortly before their wedding, and now he was trapped in depression and loneliness.

> *Faith enjoys a sunny day as much as anyone, but faith earns its keep on the gray days.*

Faith enjoys a sunny day as much as anyone, but faith earns its keep on the gray days. For it is when we know our "sins and griefs," our "trials and temptations," and feel the whip of those who "despise" us, that turning in faith to God becomes our lifeline. We cannot stop or start the rain, we cannot vanquish the hard-hearted, we cannot force reality to dance along, we cannot—no matter how we try—we cannot save ourselves. All we can do is "take it to the Lord in prayer."

I suppose that is why I find it so offensive when Christians fight each other over doctrine and morality. Jesus gave us just the one commandment—"love one another"—but we cannot let it go at that. We want perfection, we want applause, we want supremacy, we want to be deemed competent and worthy in the eyes of others.

Enough of such soupy mud. As an English preacher named Edward Mote wrote in 1834 and read to a friend's dying wife, "My hope is built on nothing less than Jesus' blood and righteousness.... On Christ the solid rock I stand."

Submission

Mark 1:9: In those days Jesus came from Nazareth of Galilee and was baptized by John in the Jordan.

I am driving home from work. My favorite radio station starts a piano piece. Suddenly, I hear the closing notes of the hymn "Abide with Me." It isn't the hymn, of course, for no classical station would stoop to playing nineteenth-century English hymns. But the mere suggestion makes me want to sing this text written by an English pastor named Henry Lyte as he was dying of tuberculosis, and the tune composed by William Monk in 1861 at a "time of great sorrow," according to his wife.

Hymns come in all flavors and get put to all uses. "Abide with Me" spans some interesting gaps: a favorite at English royal weddings, a season-ending ritual at the English football championship, and a favorite of Mohandas Gandhi.

Whatever their use elsewhere, I find myself drawn more and more to hymns like "Abide with Me," "It Is Well with My Soul," and "Now the Silence." They speak of submission to God and therefore of sadness, humility, helplessness ("help of the helpless, O abide with me") and a confidence that God is larger than anything, even tuberculosis, civil strife, death at sea, and the noise of warring nations.

I don't feel helpless most of the time. But sometimes I do. I watch the nation I love descend into imperial swagger abroad and a mean-spirited plutocracy at home. Hubris is running amok. So is casual cruelty. The strong prey on the weak, the determined exploit the uncertain, and the privileged mistake good fortune for virtue.

A window of goodness seems to be closing. For a time—what, four decades?—we thought better of our lynchings, closed doors, and glass ceilings. We didn't exactly break out in kindness and equity, but there was a visionary atmosphere, a perspective, a self-restraint, a feeling that at long last the "American Dream" was open to all.

Now wealth is being concentrated in the hands of a few, corporations are controlled by the rapacious, the prevailing religious attitudes are haughty and politicized, doors of opportunity are closing to people of color, citizens are being fed lies by politicians who have more attitude than vision, and we are embroiled in foreign conflicts that we aren't given the opportunity to understand.

The hymns that I enjoyed a decade ago—"Lift High the Cross," "Christ Is Made the Sure Foundation"—now sound too boastful to my ear. It is time to submit to God, not to boast of ourselves as right-opinioned equal partners with God.

It is time to remember that Jesus began his ministry by submitting to John the Baptist and ended it by submitting to his accusers. Pestered by the weak to become like other warriors, Jesus launched no empires—ecclesiastical, political, or media—but accepted John's baptism and went on to drown in the sorrows of a troubled land.

People then, as now, saw ways they considered more promising: armed might, proud institution, and wealth. But for Jesus, if there would be victory, it would be from God, not from armor or empire. ("Where is death's sting? where, grave, thy victory? I triumph still, if thou abide with me.")

I yearn to sing of submission to God who has seen these destructive parades before and hasn't yet lost faith in humanity.

Submission is out of fashion. No one wants to back down. Politicians behave like medieval theologians, conjuring sterile theories in safe places, without benefit of reality, not to mention actual prayer, and then forcing them on the loyal as a test of loyalty.

The cardinal virtues of what Jesus did do—inclusion, gentleness, courage, wisdom, compassion —are deemed worthless. The public stage belongs now to the elitist, monochromatic, hard-edged, the weak bully, the foolish and small-minded. Religion is made a weapon. And so I yearn to sing of submission to a God who has seen these destructive parades before and hasn't yet lost faith in humanity.

Everyone

Luke 15:31-32: [Jesus said], "Then the father said to [the elder brother], 'Son, you are always with me, and all that is mine is yours. But we had to celebrate and rejoice, because this brother of yours was dead and has come to life; he was lost and has been found.' "

I don't expect to win our office pool in college basketball's national championships. My goal is modest: not to come in last again. So far so good. As of Saturday night, I am third from last. It looks promising for Monday morning rehashing. One of our local teams is still alive; another plays today and is favored. If Kentucky will just lose, all will be right with the world of basketball.

Spoken, of course, like a true fan. For beyond peewee league, sports is about winning and losing. The college tourney starts with 65 teams and relentlessly eliminates all but one. It is a mirror of life. The hallways of life are littered with the dashed dreams of those who didn't make cheerleader, didn't get the job, didn't make the sale, couldn't afford their dream house.

For my team to win, everyone else must lose. It is fine to give every child a prize at the soccer banquet, but out there, where only the fittest survive, we recognize such softness for what it is: a denial of reality. Or so the story goes, shaping expectations and making sports perhaps our primary metaphor for life.

It certainly has become our metaphor for salvation. Some win, some lose. Winning goes to those who join the right team (Christianity), practice hard (Religion), overcome adversity (Evil), follow the rules (Good), and listen to the coach (God). All others lose.

We disagree over who belongs on the team, but rarely do we doubt that our team will win. The idea that Muslims might have equal access to God is bizarre to many Christians. How could that possibly be? What about the "narrow gate"? If God plays no favorites, what is the point of belonging? If anyone can enter heaven, why obey the rules? If the game doesn't reward winners, why try?

A reader asks, "Will God save everyone?" I certainly hope so. If any of the common metaphors for salvation are true—sports, warfare, competitive romance, academic tenure—then I am doomed. So are we all. For in the end, we all lose. Our prowess might be strong today, but teams change, skills fade, and next season might be a disaster. Winning one war just sets the stage for the next. None of us can remain young forever. Someone always knows more. Even Wal-Mart will follow Woolworth onto the slag-heap of history.

On its own evidence, life is pessimistic. Things wind down. If we learned nothing else last century, with its wars, depression, Holocaust and nuclear terror, fairness is a conceit of the temporarily successful. To link God with such momentary fairness is a cruel pathway to despair.

> Our hope lies in the mercy and grace of God.

Our hope doesn't lie in victory, not even in those victories associated with religion. Our hope lies in the mercy and grace of God. Not when God applies the standards that we would apply, or when God parcels out rewards and punishment as we imagine fairness would dictate, but when God is God, when God does what God wants to do, when God loves all that God has made, when God sees the sinner afar off and rushes to greet him, when God takes the side of the harlot, when God touches the leper, when God feeds everyone, even the betrayer, and when God looks with tenderness on humanity.

We wouldn't behave that way. We would be like the elder son, applying more rigorous standards, always separating sheep from goat and feeling justified in doing so. But we aren't God. The elder son doesn't determine the father's love.

Tomb

Luke 24:1-3: On the first day of the week, at early dawn, they came to the tomb, taking the spices that they had prepared. They found the stone rolled away from the tomb, but when they went in, they did not find the body.

My wife says later that I look bored or disgruntled, but in fact my inner pilgrim is working hard to sift and sort stray insights in Sunday school class. Walking the bridge between Scripture and life is never as easy as some people try to make it. Pat answers like historic doctrines and popular formulas never seem enough.

If the opponents of Jesus then were Romans, Zealots, Sadducees, and Pharisees, who are his opponents in my world? If they thought themselves faithful to God and protective of abiding value, are today's faithful and protective any less disturbed by God's reality, any less likely to resist a gospel that makes all things new? If they were clinging to privilege, are we also clinging and therefore rendered blind?

We can't just watch Jesus die and think we have seen enough. We have to ask why and then carry that why into our lives. I don't believe a once-and-for-all atonement was God's aim—lots of vicarious blood to wash in—but like everything else about Jesus, *The Passion of the Christ* was an invitation to see today. Not to put yesterday's events on a big screen, but to overcome the blindness that constrains our lives today and makes us mean; not a period piece expressed in authentic attire and language, but a living goad, reminder, prod, shaft of light, whisper of hope.

My pilgrim's toil continues in worship. Centerpiece is the choir's performance of *The Seven Last Words of Christ*, by Theodore Dubois. Old hat to some perhaps but new to my ears, this contemporary setting succeeds in disturbing and softening, leading not to shouts of rage or release, but quiet contemplation of sorrow, loss, submission, and hope.

Easter Day began at a tomb. It began in the inescapable reality of death. It began at early dawn when grieving women came on a grim assignment. It began in an oppressed land, where cruel Rome cared little for human life, and religious hierarchs sputtered claims of certainty that always seemed to benefit them.

"Help me see," we ask Jesus. That is God's fondest desire. Proud religion talks of victory. But Jesus wanted people to see. He touched eyes, he taught minds, he spoke against "blind guides." After Easter he appeared to his disciples so that, in seeing, they might have courage and faith.

Seeing Jesus means many things, some delightful, some perplexing, some irritating, some encouraging. The pilgrim's road is a highway of many moods. But it leads inexorably to tombs. The tomb where they placed Jesus, and the many tombs that mark our lives, from the literal death of loved ones and eventually our own lives, to the painful death of love, relationships, careers, hopes, and health, to the admittedly necessary but still difficult death of pride, appetite, and cruelty.

> *The tomb of Jesus was found empty, and so will our tombs be found empty.*

Things die, and not just the things whose death warms our hearts, but also things we hold dear and wish could live forever. The Easter promise, the ground of all faith and hope, is that not a single one of those deaths can separate us from God. The tomb of Jesus was found empty, and so will our tombs be found empty.

But to embrace any of that, we must come and see. We must cast aside blindness, especially that blindness which makes us feel safe and large. We must engage reality—not entertainment claiming to be real, but the less cinema-worthy pathways that we walk.

When we see the stone rolled away, we will be confused. The darkness proclaims death as all. But when we look inside, the body will be gone.

PART FIVE

Journey to Faith

Life isn't a static puzzle to be unlocked, but a journey to be undertaken.

God is our Companion.

Perspective

John 6:14-15: When the people saw the sign that [Jesus] had done, they began to say, "This is indeed the prophet who is to come into the world." When Jesus realized that they were about to come and take him by force to make him king, he withdrew again to the mountain by himself.

Disney World works for some convention-goers and not for others. Our resort hotel, located between the Magic Kingdom and Epcot Center, is teeming with young families eager for adventure. Children wearing mouse ears bubble in excitement.

When asked about their afternoon at the Magic Kingdom, a couple without children say, "Too many strollers." Plus one-hour waits for the best rides.

A visitor from Norway scans the massive dolphins atop our hotel, the swans atop another, huge fountains on the roofs, a manmade lake and beach, and precision-edged lawns, and says, "This is like a prison with no bars."

To find a non-Disney store selling water for less than $4.50 a bottle, one must drive fifteen miles, another conferee says. Our hotel complex supports seven restaurants (plus room service) by making it difficult to get anywhere else.

And yet as I leave a pleasant outdoor supper and walk around the lake in cool night air to my comfortable hotel room, I realize it would be churlish of me to complain. Whether this feels like prison or paradise, it is a far cry from the truly harsh and dangerous regions of our war-torn planet.

There comes a time, in other words, to seek perspective. Climb a taller hill, look farther away, consider someone else's situation, accept the day's news as reality and not entertainment and seek to know oneself. Or if self-knowledge seems elusive, at least allow the possibility that one's precision-edged persona isn't entirely real.

This Disney hotel, for example, is a victory of "Why Not? Architecture." If you can construct a two-story scallop shell and place it atop a building with a yellow-lighted fountain, why not do it? If you can put carousel stripes everywhere, why not do it? If you can take multiple architectural motifs—triangle, barrel vault, Louisiana ironwork, cloth-draped rotunda, promenade, cabana, balcony, three-tiered fountain—and make them all oversized and merge them in a single fantasy, why not do it?

> *After his feeding of the five thousand, Jesus faced a crisis of perspective. People took the wrong message from his miracle.*

It takes restraint to attain perspective. Not everything need be done just because it can be done.

After his feeding of the five thousand, Jesus faced a crisis of perspective. People took the wrong message from his miracle. They wanted to make him king. That must have felt intoxicating. Human history tells of countless able and visionary leaders who got drunk on success, acclaim, and power, and became, first, a parody and, then, a danger.

Jesus sensed the danger and fled from it. His ministry wasn't to become a king. He was a teacher, a lover, a rebel, a gatherer— many things, but not a king, not a messiah as the people expected. He used language like "Son of Man" and images like "suffering servant."

Religion always struggles with perspective. In order to justify its beliefs, religion declares other belief systems erroneous. Many Christians refuse to accept Islam, for example, as another pathway to God. In their view, there can be just one "King of kings and Lord of lords." But Jesus himself never sought such titles or such singularity.

Oh, we can always find stray quotes that justify exclusivity, but the larger message of Jesus' ministry was different. He pointed the way to God and said that if people followed him they would see God. But when zealots tried to take that too far—to build a massive rooftop scallop shell, as it were—he went away from them.

Normal

John 12:20-21: Among those who went up to worship at the festival were some Greeks. They came to Philip, who was from Bethsaida in Galilee, and said to him, "Sir, we wish to see Jesus."

After a business meeting, needing fresh air and exercise, I venture away from my hotel to "The Boardwalk." After four days in Disney World, I know what to expect: a re-creation of someplace else, idealized and made large, with well-crafted vistas and ample opportunities to shop.

Thus I find a wooden boardwalk reminiscent of Atlantic City, a dancehall playing big band music, an old-time bakery promising fresh bread, a "general store," a sports bar, "villas" and a "yacht club." All of this surrounds a small lake, where sandy beaches have "No Swimming" signs and a tour boat traces a small circle.

I am glad to be outdoors. Halfway around the lake, however, as I scan a designer's painstaking vista and try to imagine what seacoast village he was emulating, I realize that if I stayed here long enough, this would begin to seem normal. Then it would be time to leave.

"Normal," you see, proves our ability to adapt. We crave equilibrium. If one equilibrium is shaken, we will find another. Forced into the hospital by illness, we will adapt to hospital routines and eventually find it difficult to leave. When business takes me to new settings, I know that within three days I will adjust, and it will seem normal to communicate with my family by telephone and e-mail, to breathe hotel air, and to stop noticing the grandiose architecture.

Anything can become normal. It now seems normal to start the day reading warfront news from Iraq, and then to scan basketball scores. What will happen when the war stops or basketball ends? Many find life empty after warfare. Some fall into depression when they leave the hospital and its routines. Many graduates struggle outside campus life.

The ministry of Jesus struggled with "normal." Each time his disciples entered into a new equilibrium, he jostled them, went apart from them, challenged them. Whenever the people got too close and seemed on the verge of reeling him into their world, Jesus did something jarring or went away to a strange place, not only to thwart their persistent desire to stand still, but to escape his own temptation to stop.

> *The ministry of Jesus struggled with "normal." Each time his disciples entered into a new equilibrium, he jostled them, went apart from them, challenged them.*

The appearance of some Greeks was such a moment. Even though the scene starts charmingly enough—"Sir, we wish to see Jesus," source of many a sermon—the larger message is how Jesus received their arrival as a signal. He saw himself becoming normal. Even the Greeks had heard about him. Now he was a destination, perhaps not as prosaic as this artificial boardwalk around an artificial lake, but less radical, less disruptive than he had intended to be.

Now, Jesus said, would come the hour of his suffering and glorification, because the power of darkness would fight back, with all weapons at hand, to restore a pleasing equilibrium. Moreover, even if the darkness simply tried to co-opt the new movement, to sell it a few Roman temples and accept crosses in the Pantheon, it was time for him to leave so that God could "drive out" the "ruler of this world."

Salvation lies not in a new normal, but in the journey away from manmade normal and toward God.

This lakeside boardwalk is phony—not damaging, not stupid, just not real. As long as we remain in tourist mode, it seems harmless. But if we stay here too long and stop seeing the artifice of well-crafted vistas, then our journey will stop, and we will become captives of the normal.

When that happens, Jesus will shake our perches to start us journeying again.

Focus

Mark 9:2-4: Jesus was transfigured before them, and his clothes became dazzling white, such as no one on earth could bleach them. And there appeared to them Elijah with Moses, who were talking with Jesus.

My day starts early. Our three-hour presentation this morning is for high stakes. Sleep eludes me. A colleague and I worked hard getting ready. Now we plow into it, all cylinders firing. For the morning, my world feels concentrated on this conference room, images projected on a screen, and two professionals striving to find the right words. It feels like one of those important sermons, when one hones every word, every image, and then bends to the task of bridging the gap between pulpit and pew.

After a postmortem lunch, I take a long walk beside San Diego Bay. I pass by a homeless woman begging for change. I snap a photo for two tourists from Ohio. I pause in a park to field a cell phone call from Chicago. I pass by hundreds of yachts, ranging from bay cruisers to lengthy craft built for open sea. Just as I am wondering what such vessels cost, I notice a for-sale sign: $549,000. From quarters in a cup to a fortune waiting for Saturday, all in a single walk.

On my return leg, I detour around the world's longest convention center—the ugliest, too, if you ask me—and walk through downtown. Nothing exceptional, other than a surprising absence of automobiles. I watch two police officers roust a vagrant sleeping in a doorway.

I step inside the Santa Fe Railroad station: a mission-style building that plays host to a steady stream of trolleys and Amtrak trains. I hear an "All Aboard" for the Surfliner to Los Angeles and watch it leave the station. I muse about hopping on board and riding north.

The world, in other words, is much larger than a sixth-floor conference room with no windows. In the "valley" where we all live, fortunes rise and fall, people see new things and old things, strangers pass with no comment, everyone tries as best they can to make their way.

In the valley, we stay within ourselves. Two tourists can't get over being from Ohio and now standing here beside the Pacific Ocean. A man sitting alone on a bench assures a far-away child that he will be home tomorrow, and says, "I love you." A parking lot attendant spends his day in a booth tending idle BMWs. A woman walks alone to her car, with that no-eye-contact stride that women must learn through experience.

When Jesus took three disciples up a hill, he gave them a concentrated look at who he was and where their lives should lead. Like a brilliant image projected on a screen, he dazzled before them. The outside world fell away, and he began to converse with heroes from ancient days.

It was difficult for Peter, James, and John to get into the moment. They struggled to set aside the vagrants and yachts and interior journeys that occupy most of life. Peter's initial response was profoundly foolish. God would need to do more to focus their attention.

> *This moment was for high stakes. If the disciples couldn't grasp the nature of Jesus and his break from the past, how could they function down below?*

But this moment was for high stakes. If the disciples couldn't grasp the nature of Jesus and his break from the past, how could they function down below? If they couldn't concentrate on this single image, what sense could anything in the valley make to them? If they couldn't know themselves as caught up in new creation, new life, a new day of breathtaking brightness, what word could they speak tomorrow?

For any walkway beside any harbor or field is going to be lined with suffering and savoring, and one's companions will always be self-directed and often lonely people. To make any difference alongside the bay, one must see reality. Sometimes, seeing requires a scary mountain.

Question

Matthew 22:14: [Jesus said], "For many are called, but few are chosen."

My weekly newspaper column draws many responses. Some take issue; others express gratitude. Every once in a while, the deep hunger that people bring to God comes forth, as in this question from a man who was raised outside the church but has read some religious books: "How can a man like you, scholarly, educated, and experienced in all the vagaries of life, embrace the notion of Jesus' divinity?"

"I am not asking for an easy answer in one neat little place," he writes, "just some suggestions as to where to look further."

Dear pilgrim, you ask a good question, and you know not to expect a simple answer. Faith isn't that easy.

Every Sunday, faithful men and women climb into pulpits carrying this very question in their hearts. Having been there myself, I know they are baffled. And if they aren't honest about being baffled, if they claim certainty and promise to say everything that needs to be said, I suggest you run for the exit.

Every day—at kitchen tables and seminary desks, on long walks and in short, desperate bedside prayers—the wise and foolish lay before God questions they can barely phrase. They are reaching for solace, hope, courage, forgiveness, peace. Some believe they receive answers, but all can know the grace of asking questions worth asking. That is so much better than asking what bauble to buy next.

Many experiences have shaped my faith, but five come especially to mind today:

First, going to church with my parents, and watching my father and mother bow their heads in prayer. The preaching was dull, the liturgy overblown, but all around me were people reaching out to God.

Second, watching a small-minded congregation beat up on a loving pastor, and yet seeing him forgive them and continue to care for them. He loved Jesus, and he loved them.

Third, reading Romans 8:12-17, where Paul says we are adopted by God, that God places a spirit in us that leads us to cry out for him, as a child cries for a parent. God loves us first.

Fourth, sitting in a seminary carrel and studying Mark 10:46-52, the healing of blind Bartimaeus, for hour after hour, until I saw that we all start blind, we all start knowing little about Jesus except his name, we all sit in the dust and cry out for healing, and Jesus hears our cry when others would go deaf.

> All can know the grace of asking questions worth asking. That is so much better than asking what bauble to buy next.

Fifth, sitting each morning as I have done for the past nine years, with the Gospels in one hand and, as you put it, the "vagaries of life" in the other, and searching for God in daily life. Not to prove or disprove the formulas of religion, not to validate any doctrine, not to stay loyal to any label or "ism," but simply to see what there is to see.

My journey won't be your journey. Religion, in my opinion, needs to back off from its triumphalist claims and acknowledge that God has provided many pathways, some grounded in Jesus and some not. One can build an institution on claiming to have the only answers, but God seems larger than that.

Where could you start your journey? You could start by taking the "vagaries of life" seriously. That is what Jesus did. You could sit with your questions and not rush to answers. You could look for a community of faith where people value searching more than finding.

You could sit alone with the Bible in one hand—starting with the Psalms or Mark—and the "vagaries of life" in the other, and just read, reflect, be puzzled, read some more. Don't try to figure it out. Just live within it. God will find you.

Self

Matthew 22:36-38: [The lawyer said], "Teacher, which commandment in the law is the greatest?" [Jesus] said to him, "You shall love the Lord your God with all your heart, and with all your soul, and with all your mind. This is the greatest and first commandment."

While the Washington D.C. sniper is picking off his thirteenth victim, a bus driver going to work, I am venturing into post–9/11 air travel: screening, identification checks, luggage searches, and a reflexive scanning of fellow passengers for shifty eyes.

While a major assault on the Internet is under way, shutting down nine of the Internet's thirteen backbone servers, I am resuming my usual workday position at a computer wired to the Internet.

While police in the D.C. area are evaluating the sniper's threat to kill children "anytime, anywhere," I am watching my eleven-year-old son play soccer in an open field ringed by numerous firing positions.

Somewhere out there are people to whom assaults on the innocent make perfect sense. Some enjoy the slaughter and its ensuing spotlight. Some believe mayhem and panic will serve their just cause. Some have made a god of their anger, and they love that god dearly.

Meanwhile, at the soccer game, the mother of the team's most selfish player goes ballistic when her son is yellow-carded for a flagrant foul. In language worthy of a sailor, she berates officials, moans dramatically to the audience, tells her shame-faced son he did nothing wrong, and is still carrying on twenty minutes later. I cannot even count the false gods ruling her life tonight.

This is the face of extremism. Not wild and crazy people frothing openly for all to see, but people who have crossed one line, two lines, and ever so subtly set themselves before the wrong throne. Forced to make their way in a perplexing world, they move from self-reliant to self-serving, from self-serving to self-centered, and from self-centered to self-worshiping. Angered by circumstance, they project their anger onto others, name the other an enemy and themselves the avenger, and in delicious righteousness, they strike. Feeling small and hating that smallness, they try to grow large by destroying others.

The scenarios are endless, but at their center is the subtle displacement of God and the enthronement of self. The sniper—probably a sad, belittled soul trying to get big through violence—is simply an extreme version of the soccer mom who has no regard for the damage she does, especially to her own son.

There are no codes of conduct that can regulate such behavior. The ancient Hebrews tried, with a legal code of bewildering complexity. Our governments try, with legal systems that choke on their volume, turf battles, and political gamesmanship. Religions try, with a legalism that never tires of finding fault.

But the issue is so basic, so far beneath the radar of code or retribution: Who is lord of your life?

> *When you are lost in anger, self-pity, or self-loathing, who will come in search of you?*

Not what brand of righteousness do you subscribe to, but when you wake up in the morning, whose bidding are you ready to do? When you venture into harm's way, whose shield protects you? When you fail, who will pick you up? When you weep, who will catch your tears? When you feel small, who will join you in your smallness? When you are lost in anger, self-pity, or self-loathing, who will come in search of you? When you mark off another day won by fatigue, who will keep watch during the night?

There are no laws that can answer such questions. No proofs, no arguments, no lists of holy attributes, no tips for holy living, no doctrines guaranteeing success, no princely authorities, no apparatus. There isn't even a decision-making process, or a first step one takes.

There is only God, who loves us first. God beyond religion, God beyond legalism, God beyond defining or controlling—God who simply is.

Samples

John 6:34-35: They said to [Jesus], "Sir, give us this bread always." Jesus said to them, "I am the bread of life. Whoever comes to me will never be hungry, and whoever believes in me will never be thirsty."

Checkout lines are long at Costco. But we are here to examine an item, not to buy. As we carry out our mission, we pass by tables offering free samples of food. Shrimp, yogurt, chicken, quesadillas, raspberry spread, olive oil, bean dip, key lime pie—each is given out in a one-bite serving, along with a brief spiel.

"We could almost eat lunch here," laughs my wife. It would be an odd lunch, but we could make the table circuit several times and eventually get full.

But these are just samples, and we know that. Lunch lies ahead at a café that claims an "upscale mountain lodge" motif, whatever that means. There we sit and talk about family things. There we encounter friends. There we get a real meal—not the only meal we will ever need, but certainly more than samples at the discount store.

Beyond our sight are people who have no food. Some are invisible neighbors; millions live far away in conditions beyond comprehension, assigned by perverse chance to sterile land and oppressive societies. Like it or not, I am connected to them.

It is possible to approach faith as if it were a sampler. An hour of worship, a Lenten study group, a morning's Habitat duty, an evening committee. Each sample has substance, each is offered as an invitation to go deeper, but in the end, a circuit of sampling stations leaves one unfilled.

Many yearn to go deeper, stay longer, discuss real things, and get food that will last. They seek out study groups, renewal communities, books and tapes, extended mission work—some even go to "upscale mountain lodges." My quest has led me to my morning writing.

Seeking more proves to be a vexing quest, not because real food is difficult to find, but because sampling is so tempting—a lark, no cost—and staying longer so disturbing.

Serious mission work can render one unfit to resume normal life. Every month's duty at the homeless shelter leaves me dazed. Sustained study of scripture can confuse one's religion. Anything that renews faith changes life. A sharing group will illuminate hidden corners. Intense prayer draws everything into question. The more I write, the less I am drawn to the tidy routines of Sunday religion.

> *Anything that renews faith changes life.*

If we want to understand what Jesus meant by "bread of life," I think we need to look beyond eucharistic practices and stale bickering over type of bread, format for feeding, rules for receiving—concerns that are little more than sample-station management.

We need to look at what happens when we venture deeper. We get confused, but we also feel God's touch. Old values get challenged, but better values emerge. Comfort seems elusive, but being comforted happens more. We feel part of something larger—threatening but enriching.

We don't become holier or less prone to error. We don't rise above the herd. If anything, we see ourselves with humbler eyes, and we feel connected to some unexpected people. We lose control, but we learn the difference between abiding joy and the shallow lark of sampling.

Most clergy and laity I know would love to get out of the sampler business and go deeper. We aren't fooled by sampler cuisine or satisfied by it. But we are stuck—in ourselves, inherited routines, and a culture that approaches everything as sampling.

I just know that "bread of life" does exist, it can be found, and it is within our capability to accept its sustenance. Jesus didn't promise something exotic, or something impossible for all but a few to locate. We just have to search for it, knowing as we search that blessing requires breaking, and when we find "bread of life," something dear to us will need to die.

A "Deal"

John 6:32-33: Jesus said to them, "Very truly, I tell you, it was not Moses who gave you the bread from heaven, but it is my Father who gives you the true bread from heaven. For the bread of God is that which comes down from heaven and gives life to the world."

Vacation beckoning, I complete two business proposals and send them off. My goal is to nurture a discussion about value. What value does each partner bring to the table? What value can each receive? What greater value—new value, not pre-existing value—is created by working together?

To answer those questions, I need to know who we are, who they are, and what the marketplace needs from us.

If this were easy, business deals would be like apples: you see one, you pick it. But discerning value is difficult. Self-knowledge is rarely complete, and knowledge of the other can be difficult to attain, for we are motivated to hide and to self-protect.

My approach is to start with informal conversation, not formalities; then to propose concepts, not specifics; then to widen the dialogue, then to draft enough specifics to make a deal, but always to know that risk will be unavoidable and consequences unpredictable.

Now, make the intuitive leap to Jesus. Yes, business metaphors are foreign to an itinerant rabbi living in premodern times. But imagine anyway.

Imagine Jesus trying to connect with the crowd. He has a "deal" to propose, a new partnership, a new entity that will bring value to them, value to him, and new value to the world.

Imagine Jesus starting with conversation—just words, maybe a few actions to underscore his words, but mainly talking and listening. He reveals himself; he listens to their self-revelation.

Imagine Jesus offering concepts—metaphorical ideas like "bread of life," images pointing beyond themselves, ways to free the mind, to touch deeper hungers and to suggest new pathways. Imagine Jesus widening the circle, bringing in more voices, more needs, stepping outside traditional boundaries to include those whom previous "contracts" had excluded.

Imagine if Jesus had had more time. Would he have gone on to specifics, laying out his new "contract," as it were, the specific expectations and behaviors that oneness with God entails? Maybe the Last Supper was a taste of those specifics, maybe the church has been right to treat that meal as definitive, as the literal contract between God and humankind. But what if Jesus was still conceptualizing, still imagining, still leading people beyond the literal, still midstream in urging his friends to think larger than mere manna?

> *What if the Last Supper was like a midpoint in a business deal: not the outcome itself but a gathering of interested parties to imagine the outcome?*

Jesus was taken away before the "deal" was defined. We were left with concepts, not specifics. Christians have taken those midstream concepts and built an institution on them. We discerned "law"—obligation, sanction, boundary—in preliminary words whose real purposes were to open minds, to bend hearts, and to draw strangers closer. We discerned "structure" in gatherings that were still informal, still being shaped. We discerned "contract"—value given, value received—in actions that were still explorations.

In other words, we jumped to conclusions about what Jesus wanted. Our conclusions might be accurate—we certainly proclaim them as such—but on balance they seem self-serving, shallow, and not much in keeping with the conversations Jesus was leading.

When Jesus said "bread of life," for example, did he mean a communion wafer, or himself, or something even larger? We have focused on eucharistic liturgy, as if that meal contained all that faith promised or required. But what if "bread of life" meant something larger and different? What if the Last Supper was like a midpoint in a business deal: not the outcome itself but a gathering of interested parties to imagine the outcome?

After all these years, all the scholarship and arguing, all the wars and turf battles, could we ever return to the table to resume an exploration that got prematurely interrupted?

Retreat

Mark 1:35: In the morning, while it was still very dark, [Jesus] got up and went out to a deserted place, and there he prayed.

After a demanding six hours of meetings, telephone calls, and e-mail, it is time to withdraw a few paces. I turn on the CD player, put on earphones, and allow Willie Nelson's epic "Stardust" album to croon away the noise and to focus my thoughts.

I like the pressure of a growing business, the sense that every minute matters. I know myself as energized by other people. But every now and then, it helps to go away to a "deserted place," a place that has been emptied.

This is more than the "recharging of batteries," which busy people often turn to religion to achieve. My batteries are charged. Like a military retreat in the face of overwhelming force, a retreat to emptied space is necessary to stay alive and healthy.

Busy people can become manic—hyperactive, disorganized, driven—and in their mania they can become destructive. They stop listening, stop reflecting, and become impatient with others. They interrupt and bluster, because delays such as someone else's opinion and needs get in the way. They work too quickly and accomplish too little. Pace, not efficacy, becomes everything. They ride hard over other people.

I remember one year when I was starting a new pastorate. I set a killer pace and bounced manically from one event to another. My Day-Timer was jammed, but before long, I was exhausted and people were irritated.

Soldiers retreat because the situation has become too hazardous. That, I think, is the issue. Not a need for more energizing, but a need to step away from danger. Retreat isn't a tactic for enhancing one's capability; retreat grows out of one's self-destructive tendencies. Retreat isn't a "self-improvement" exercise; it is a confession of weakness.

Why did Jesus retreat to a deserted place? To understand his retreat, we should examine what happens to leaders when they get on a roll. They get swelled heads. They stop seeing other people as worthy. They begin to think themselves superior, invincible, all-knowing and even godlike. They strut when they should stop to listen. They maneuver people into harm's way in order to accomplish personal objectives. They become isolated, cruel, and eventually foolish and absurd.

Jesus went on retreat because he had just been idolized by a throng. If he listened too avidly to the crowd's applause, he would lose himself. He needed to step away from that danger—as he did often in his ministry, usually after a success—and put himself in a position to listen to God. For in the end, his life—like all of our lives—was to be about servanthood, not mastery; self-denial, not self-promotion; healing, not ruling.

> We need to see the seductions in applause and the folly in comfort.

To regain that focus, to understand purposes larger than busy days and mounting fame, he needed to step away from the noise that he himself was generating. So do we all. My retreat into a crooner's soothing is only a palliative. I won't truly escape the danger until I enter an emptied place.

Retreats aren't difficult to find. I remember a hard-charger who spent an hour each week just holding sick babies at a hospital. Quiet church pews can be a retreat. So can listening to a troubled child or serving a hungry person. My wife goes for walks and talks to neighbors. I play golf, truly a mindless activity where my success drive will invariably be defeated. My morning time of prayer and writing starts earlier and earlier, as my need for emptying grows.

The challenge, I think, is to recognize the danger. Even in full stride, we need enough self-awareness to recognize our mania, our overbearing behavior, or our excessive demands and impatience. We need to see the seductions in applause and the folly in comfort.

Camp

Mark 6:34: As [Jesus] went ashore, he saw a great crowd; and he had compassion for them, because they were like sheep without a shepherd.

On our drive to camp, we pass through a city that became a wilderness to me, with harsh treatment, unexpected suffering, abundant grace, lessons learned the hard way, reexamined values, and a transformed relationship with God.

Then on to the mountains and summer camp. Joining a long line waiting to enter camp, we park near the carefully landscaped entrance to a gated community. I tell my eleven-year-old son that this pretty tableau isn't what the mountains are like. I point instead to a steep hillside dark and wild with pines, oaks, and rhododendron.

My son is nervous, as even grownups are nervous when facing the new. I sense him scanning each face, each detail of the drop-off process, his cabin, the empty bunks, and unfamiliar counselor. He has done this before, so he knows not to panic. Even so, this isn't a walk on manicured grass.

My wife and I say goodbye, leaving our son to make his own bed. When camp ends, he will be sorry to leave. But today I see in his face what I often sense in my own when facing the new and challenging: "What am I doing here?"

What do I wish for him?

I don't wish a carefully landscaped world, which tames the wilderness with grassy vistas imported from suburbia. I don't wish a gate that keeps out whatever feels dangerous. I don't wish sanitized adventures.

I want him to know the transformation of a "deserted place" into a welcoming place. I want him to love the mountains, not to dream of taming them with bulldozer and grass. I want him to make new friends by daring to engage. I want him to try new things, even if he fails at mastery. I want him to learn more about himself by venturing farther beyond the mirror of his parents' eyes.

I know that day one will mean loneliness and false starts. But then will come day two. I want him to know how that new day dawned brighter.

Whether we are protecting our children or ourselves, I think we become too concerned with bulldozing and gating. Yes, the mountains are wild. So is most of life. We are surrounded by the weak and self-serving, and at times we take our place in their cruel ranks.

No matter how diligent our landscaping, creation won't be tamed. We must learn to treasure creation, not to master it. No matter how carefully we arrange our hair, wardrobes, credentials, and defenses, each day will be a challenge. We must learn to embrace challenge, not to avoid it.

When Jesus led his weary disciples to a deserted place to rest, a crowd of seekers followed them. Rather than send them away as an unplanned nuisance, Jesus had "compassion." His compassion took the form, first, of teaching—presumably the very teachings that challenged others, led some to turn against him, and caused the religious establishment to reject him. No safety here, for student or for teacher.

> *Jesus needed them to know how they made it: by grace, not by mastery or by avoidance.*

His compassion then turned to feeding them—in a way that would challenge his disciples' preconceptions and require the hungry to sit "in groups of hundreds and fifties," like campers being assigned to cabins.

At the end of the day, the people would be fed to fullness. But that wasn't the main point. For they would be hungry again tomorrow. Jesus needed them to know how they made it: by grace, not by mastery or by avoidance.

That is what I wish for my son at camp, that he will learn to see grace—not the prettiness of a manicured lawn, but by the grace of God, light and life in the wilderness.

Work

Acts 2:11: [The people said], "In our own languages we hear them speaking about God's deeds of power."

Moving day starts early. It is raining, of course. Sons show up, plus a girlfriend. We start carrying items such as books and kitchenware, while professional movers haul furniture. Soon, both old and new houses are a jumble of stuff and Carolina clay.

The pristine new house we bought yesterday becomes a home, starting with clutter and continuing on to pushing one car out of soupy red clay, making snap decisions about what goes where, and, at day's end, baptizing our new screen porch with Chinese carryout and laughter.

For a time, even the simplest things will be difficult. Telephone service comes Monday and Internet cable in two weeks. Who knows when newspaper and mail will find us?

But what an adventure! Ten months in the making, this project strained what little patience I possess. But here we are, a family sitting on the porch, exhausted but glowing.

As we close up for the night, I thank my twenty-two-year-old son. "You are a good worker," I tell him. "You know how to work." I marvel at each member of my family and their capacity for work. I notice that my oldest son's girlfriend matches him effort for effort. I think sometimes that our family was born too late, into an age of leisure, whereas our souls are constituted for farming.

I wonder if leisure suits any of us. Having too much too easily can make us soft, and the soft eventually become cruel. I wonder if the mounting intolerance of our age reflects the self-loathing that infects the idle. Would terrorists spring up so readily if unemployment were not so high? Would urban gangs find recruits if young men had jobs? Would "country club slackers" find such easy sledding in politics if the common sense that arises from hard work were more prevalent?

I remember a Lakota Sioux named Donny, who left the reservation for Chicago. He made it, but the rewards—leisure time and possessions—never seemed enough. He returned to the reservation, to poverty and hard work. I met him while shingling a church. I had degrees and relative wealth. But I would rather have Donny's respect than gold. One day he told me, "You know how to work."

The Hebrews understood their God as a worker. The Greeks might worship idlers who played and squabbled on a mountain. But Yahweh was a gardener, planter, pioneer, settler, builder, potter.

Spare me your solemn assemblies, said Yahweh, your idle priestly caste, your women of leisure whom Amos termed "cows of Bashan." The formative tension in the Old Testament was between city and countryside, between temple (Jerusalem) and shrine (Shechem), between a settled way of life grounded in rules and a nomadic existence grounded in family.

> *I wonder if leisure suits any of us. Having too much too easily can make us soft, and the soft eventually become cruel.*

That tension continues in our day. Farmers regard bankers and grain buyers as predators who get rich on others' toil. Small shopkeepers don't trust big business, where cleverness wins and community spirit is for suckers. In the military, enlisted troops obey their college-educated officers, but it is the master sergeants and senior chiefs whom they respect. Classroom teachers have little use for central office bureaucrats.

These historic tensions are revealing. They suggest a fundamental human value, namely, that work matters, effort matters, obligations matter, steadfast tending of soil matters, feeling tired and useful at day's end matters. Work takes many forms, but not having work can cripple the soul.

On the Day of Pentecost, inspired disciples proclaimed a God known in "deeds of power." Not a fickle deity toying with humankind, not a resident of temple or stickler for protocols, but a worker-God, a God who entered into creation's toil.

Re-invent

Mark 14:61-62: The high priest asked [Jesus], "Are you the Messiah, the Son of the Blessed One?" Jesus said, "I am; and 'you will see the Son of Man seated at the right hand of the Power,' and 'coming with the clouds of heaven.'"

Midway through this meeting I mount a soapbox. Not because the topic—project management training—is inherently passionate, but because the larger context stirs my blood.

As we interview two trainers from a local college, I am listening for signs of rigidity versus flexibility, textbook versus creativity. Will they offer the standard thirty-five hours of Project Management Institute training, or help us think and re-invent?

I draw three boxes on the whiteboard. One box says, "Tell me what to do." These are people who respond to assignments or challenges by saying, "Tell me the rules," "Tell me my duties," "Tell me the boundaries."

The second box says, "I know what I already know." These are people who already have the answers, or want to appear so. They cite authoritative sources. They filter fresh ideas through existing knowledge. They resist discovery.

The third box says, "Think, Create, Re-invent." This isn't really a box, but an absence of box. My bias, I tell them, is that we must always "re-invent the wheel." That attitude infuriates the boundary-seekers and authority-citers. But I believe there is always a better way to do something, always a fresh interpretation, always a responsibility to think for ourselves.

I am not interested in "cookie-cutter" training, I tell them. I don't want our staff to be memorizing PMI methods. We need our own methods, and, above all, we need an ability to think creatively about the problem at hand. If this training can help us to think, I am all for it. But if it stifles creativity under the weight of someone else's "best practices," forget it.

As I sit down, I observe my soapbox. Where did that passion come from? It came from eighteen years of serving congregations where fresh and creative thinking—about anything, from Scripture to worship to office layout—was not only loathed but actively resisted. "We don't need to re-invent the wheel" is another form of the "seven last words of the church."

Our fundamental human duty, I believe, is to think and re-invent, not to memorize and replicate. The best training is always a question, not an answer. I ache when I see the stifling of curiosity and creativity in my sons' schools. As a Bible teacher, I die inside when surrounded by passivity and an attitude of "tell me what it means."

Jesus was a blasphemer. He was a radical, a rebel. He had no use for the boxes of traditional religion, and we Christians have done him a tragic disservice by placing him inside boxes labeled "doctrine" and "tradition."

> *Let's recognize our passivity as driven by fear and not by God's call.*

When asked if he was "the Messiah," he said, "I am," but he went on to explain what he meant by that: not what they meant, and not what the ancients meant. He meant something new. He meant what he was in the process of living out: not a cookie-cutter, but a dynamic way of interacting with reality.

Christian religion, it seems to me, is trapped inside the first box: "Tell me what to do." We call it "faithful" and "orthodox," but let's be honest: we're scared and passive. We are scared of what our lives would be like if we truly encountered the Son of God, and if we then truly encountered the Prince of Darkness, and if we then truly encountered the world as it is, and if we then truly created a new future.

We ought to be scared. The box-less life is frightening. But let's recognize our passivity as driven by fear and not by God's call. And let's pray for courage and not for better cookie-cutters.

Trip

Luke 15:20: [Jesus said, The younger son] "set off and went to his father. But while he was still far off, his father saw him and was filled with compassion; he ran and put his arms around him and kissed him."

I am sitting at a departure gate, waiting to put my twelve-year-old son onto his first transcontinental flight. He will be retrieved 3,000 miles later by his uncle.

I am nervous. It is no small thing to put a child onto an airplane, to start him on a journey of many miles, a journey further into maturity. He will be changed by this trip. Seeing new places, spending a weekend with another family, traveling by himself, and having internal adventures beyond my imagining will bring him home a new boy.

I try to imagine what the father in Jesus' parable felt when his son went away. Did he already know his son was weak, a wastrel in the making? Did he see the grabbing of inheritance for what it was? Did he imagine the best, the worst? Did he lie awake nights?

I picture him as sorrowful. Not sorry to see the child become a man, for that is a necessary journey, but sorry to see critical stages in that journey happening beyond his sight, on shaky ground, beyond his capacity to help. Maybe he wondered what his son was experiencing. Maybe he just missed him.

When I pick up my son on Monday, I will be looking for his face. Not a report card on how he behaved, not an account of his adventures, not his learnings or frustrations. Those will come in time. But first I will look for his face, the sight of him drawing near. That will be my joy.

I wonder if we could ever understand God in that way? As compassionate, as so eager to see us that God runs and embraces.

That is how Jesus portrays God in his parable. That is how Jesus treated people. I believe that is how Jesus expects us to treat one another.

Not the scorekeeping God proclaimed by those who love rules and punishments. Not the grudge-holding God of those who cannot forgive. Not the controlling God who determines all things. Not the triumphalist God who sees the sinner repenting and shouts, "Gotcha!" Not any of those faces of God that have been lifted up over the centuries by the angry, unforgiving, controlling, legalistic, and frightened.

Jesus proclaimed a God who yearns for the sight of us, who is so thrilled at seeing us draw near that, abandoning the prerogatives of the indignant parent, God sees us from far away and rushes to greet us.

> *Jesus spoke of a God who never ceases to scan the horizon, looking for our return.*

How did we ever get so wasteful of God that we proclaimed God as little more than an extension of ourselves? Judgmental, in the way we dismiss and disparage. Score-minded, in the way we track every failing of others. Harsh, in the way we are cold. Legalistic, in the way we want to control the calculus of grace.

Who would want to go home to a God like that? A reader asks how she can get closer to God. The first step is to imagine God as wanting her close. The second is to start moving. The third is to see God's smile and outstretched arms, and to run into those arms, not in defeat, not in humiliation, not in any return to the smallness of childhood, but in gladness—in God's gladness and in her own.

Jesus spoke of a God who never ceases to scan the horizon, looking for our return.

Scripture Index